D1563494

"Every choice we make can be a celebration of the world we want." Frances Moore Lappé

World Class

Published in the United States by ReinventED, Sheviron, LLC, NY, 2010.

Cover design & illustrations by Mary Ellen Kalil Shevalier

Cartoon illustration designed with TOONDOO by Françoise Piron www.toondoo.com (pp. 94-95)

Nature photography by Mark T. Shevalier

Photos by:

Virginia Davey (p. 9)
Sue Hochmuth (p. 41)
Mary Ellen Shevalier (p. 8, p. 27, p. 167)

Text set in 11 point Georgia
This book is available at a special discount for bulk purchases in the U.S. by corporations, institutions, and other organizations. For more information contact ReinventED, 5870 Nutting Street Road, Henderson, NY 13650, or e-mail worldclassbook@gmail.com.

Copyright data is available from the Library of Congress
United States Copyright Office

ISBN 978-0-615-42228-2

First Edition

10 9 8 7 6 5 4 3 2 1

World Class

The Re-education of America

Françoise Piron and Mary Ellen Shevalier

with research contributed by Lisa Parsons

Edited by Virginia E. Davey

Authors' Definition

We* (wē) *pron. pl.* : students, teachers, parents, administrators, neighbors, business leaders, university presidents, professors, future teachers, policy makers, State Commissioners of Education, U.S. Secretary of Education, U.S. Secretary of State, President of the United States of America, all world leaders, me, you, us, them, ALL.

Everyone is talking about educational reform.

How can we* change the current educational system to include and *value* all students?

It is fundamental and attainable.

We* have the answer within us.

This book offers a universal equation for education. It is right for all ages and subjects, as long as *we** are not afraid to embrace its message.

Dedicated to our mothers,

Mary Kalil and Nicole Piron;

our first, best, and most important teachers.

You instilled respect, nurtured love,

and promoted

peace in our hearts.

To all my past and present students, thank you for all you have taught me. I hope to honor you by using the lessons of the past to benefit those who will follow in our footsteps.

Mary Ellen Shevalier

Special gratitude to the South Jefferson Central School District, in particular Mrs. Jamie Moesel, Superintendent of Schools; Mrs. Karen Denny, High School Principal; Mrs. Heidi Edgar, Guidance Counselor; and Mrs. RaeAnn Thomas, Technology Leader. Thank you for believing in us and supporting our amazing journey.

Swaz Piron

World Class

A preface by Dr. Jacquelyn S. Kibbey, Ph.D.
S.U.N.Y. Oswego*

Don't you just hate stereotypes? So do the amazing women who authored this book!

In fact, this book shatters the stereotypical belief that mature teachers, who are closer to the end of their careers than the beginning – are burnt out, are out of touch with the reality of the current world and generation, and are always looking to take the easy way out. This couldn't be further from the truth! In fact, these two women are some of the most innovative and dynamic teachers I have met in a long time – and I've met a lot of teachers throughout my 30 year career!

This is an amazing story. It takes place in the North Country (upstate New York, near Canada), in a rural school that is located near Fort Drum,** the U.S. army base, home of the 10th Mountain Division. The authors are caring women who have invested a great deal in their professions because they care so deeply about their students. Mary Ellen and Swaz don't accept that things can't be done because there is no money for it or because there is no precedent for it in schools. Instead, their students always come first as they invent, convince, search, implement, and manipulate whatever is in their students' best interests.

Mary Ellen and Françoise are cutting edge teachers as they dive headlong into the areas of interdisciplinary curriculum development, technology, team teaching, global communication, at-risk students, multi-age grouping, and curriculum relevancy. The culmination of all of their efforts has resulted in the delivery of a landmark course entitled, "I am a Citizen of the World."

These innovative teachers have shared their ability to garner administrative support, funding, community interest, and student input through amazing course offerings that have drawn students and their studies into the 21st century. Mary Ellen and Françoise have not been reluctant to use technology or to collaborate with others as needed to achieve their educational goals. Together, they have invented a unique type of course focusing on media literacy. It is both relevant and timely. Please read along to see how their adventure unfolded. I have been privileged to observe Mary Ellen and Swaz firsthand and I am still amazed by what they have accomplished and continue to accomplish. They have managed to bring about much needed change in the field of education. World Class is a great guide for all educators who continue to follow their dreams and build upon their experiences. It is also for those teachers who wish to give back to their fields and to make their classrooms come to life. All schools should be lucky enough to have teachers with this much courage and enthusiasm. Here is to teachers with passion, dreams, and innovation. May they be an inspiration to us all!

* Jacquelyn Kibbey, *Associate Professor, Curriculum & Instruction* at SUNY Oswego; BA, MA, PhD, Ohio State U. Appointed 1990
1988 NATIONAL ART EDUCATION ASSOCIATION Higher Education Division Regional Awards
Art Coordinator for the Fairbanks Public School District, Fairbanks Alaska.

** Fort Drum is a U.S. Army military reservation in Jefferson County, New York, United States. The population was 12,123 at the 2000 census. It is home to the 10th Mountain Division. Its mission is to support active and reserve units from all services in training at Fort Drum, and planning and support for the mobilization and training of almost 80,000 troops annually.
http://en.wikipedia.org/wiki/Fort_Drum

A note from the authors: Mary Ellen Shevalier

I remember finally receiving my license to teach in 1982. That was almost thirty years ago. I felt proud and honored to be called a teacher. I still feel this way. It is a privilege to serve my country and my community by serving our children. When I first started my teaching career, little did I know that the historical, hierarchical structure of educational systems predisposes educational institutions to inherent inequities. This book contains stories that expose my frustrations over an educational system whose history of demoralizing restrictions have stifled the individual strengths and innovations of its administration, its teachers, and consequently, its clients. These stories illustrate what I consider to be an obsolete, largely ineffectual, and prejudicial educational system. Yet, as many of my colleagues would admit, we are still grateful for the positive intent of the American Public School System.

My many journals of these stories have been quietly tucked away over the years. They now call out to be shared with a mission of propelling the educational changes that are so desperately needed in the 21st century. The timing could not be more perfect. Educational reform is becoming the hottest topic of our time. It is a hot topic because it has been simmering (or stewing) for years! We know that we are products of this system. I optimistically view this as a time in history when we will record the greatest systemic transformation since the inception of the public school system. Just this week (November, 2010) Katie Couric, news anchor of the CBS Evening News, ran a weeklong series on the topic of *Reading, Writing, and Reform.* Also, this same week, Oprah Winfrey, world famous talk show personality, hosted a panel of government, business, and educational leaders who echoed the importance of educational reform. I was impressed by the benevolence of Mark Zuckerberg, the 26 year old CEO of Facebook, when he made a substantial, personal and financial, investment to assist the educational reform movement. Ironically, Zuckerberg said that he had been seriously thinking about educational reform for the past year. He proceeded to tell a story about one of his employees who had caused the entire Facebook site to crash. Can you believe the company celebrated his "risk–taking" attitude by having a party? Zuckerberg indicated that his company rewards risk-taking as well as moving expeditiously. He considers these the two actions that propel us forward. I laughed at the irony of his statement in contrast to my own journaling for almost three decades! One thing is for certain, the time *is* ripe for combining our knowledge, energy, and commitment to make the necessary educational changes.

This book has been written because I believe deeply in the impact that education can have on our quality of life on a local, national, and global scale. I began my career by thinking that I was a teacher who specialized in a specific content area. I now know that I am a teacher of children, your children and our children! The day that this shift in paradigm occurred was the first day that my eyes were opened to the profoundly awesome responsibility that our profession bestows upon its teachers. This responsibility is one that I, and millions of other teachers, willingly assume each and every day. We are hopeful that our perseverance will positively influence the life of each child in our classrooms. We hope that many more students, in turn, will be impacted by the outcomes of our collective contributions. For all of my colleagues who feel the same way, the antidote is within our reach. As I near the end of my career in the classroom, I now know that teaching has been much more than a profession. It has been my life's vocation. Throughout this book, I share my observations and experiences as a teacher in America. Perhaps even more importantly, this book offers some answers that are concrete yet modifiable. Some of these pages provide an educational equation that is universal. It can be implemented immediately. Indeed, the time has come to recognize and embrace our undeniable global connectedness. It is my hope that our experiences, as illustrated throughout <u>World class, The Re-education of America</u> will awaken all of us to the importance of the movement intended to mend our broken educational system. I believe it is time.

Swaz Piron

We should write such a book because...

our children are the future leaders of this planet.

ideas are more important than information.

the world is flatter than ever.

two brains are better than one.

there is so much wasted talent.

we are ready for authentic education.

the paradigms have changed.

we are losing our children.

we desperately need independent thinkers.

our students want to be heard.

we want to be competitive in this global economy.

our students are digital natives.

good group work leads to quality projects.

we need to embrace our differences.

understanding others is key.

the world needs problem solvers.

World Class

we need to focus on our strengths and minimize the negative impact of our weaknesses.

I am blue-green and you are orange.

our students deserve better.

we want our kids to become citizens of the world.

we love our children, our country, and our world too much not to share what we know.

Do you...

care about the future of our children?

think that school is not adapted to the needs of current learners?

agree that on our planet everything and everyone is interconnected?

feel that education could be a lot more fun, a lot more relevant, and a lot more democratic than it is presently?

see a disconnect between schools and the real world?

find unacceptable the current high school dropout rate of 30%*?

*http://edlabor.house.gov/newsroom/2009/05/high-school-dropout-crisis-thr.shtml

If you answered yes to any of the above questions, please READ ON and start to contribute to the re-education of America.

World Class

TABLE OF CONTENTS

CHAPTER 1

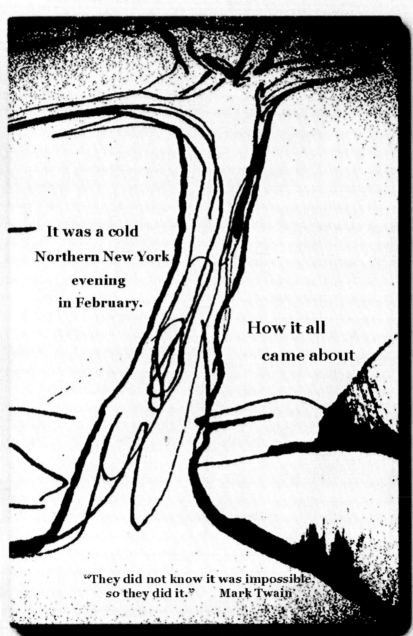

It was a cold
Northern New York
evening
in February.

How it all
came about

"They did not know it was impossible,
so they did it."   Mark Twain

Reflection: Mary Ellen- February 2008

She sat next to me during a school concert. It was a benefit for cancer research, a night called "Celebration of Life." In between songs, my principal leaned over and said, "Wouldn't it be great if you could teach a course like the Positive News Now activity that you did last year [referring to an extracurricular program that was intended to promote positive character and the heralding of good deeds throughout the school]?" My heart jumped, a smile slid across my face, and my eyes opened wide as I enthusiastically whispered back, "Oh, if you only knew what I've been thinking. We will talk." The next song began.

The following day, we were gifted with a snow day. I drafted a four year vision for a new course of study that I fully intended to use as the impetus to change our educational practices. It was to be called, "I am a Citizen of the World" (a course of study in media literacy and social issues). The convergence of time, energy, and vision was no coincidence. It was rather an answer to over a decade of thought, prayer, and journaling of ideas. I call it a *God-incidence*.

Journal entry: Mary Ellen – February 1999

I ponder my life's journey in education and realize it brings me back to memories of when I was five years old. On the six-by-eight foot, screened-in porch of our inner city upstairs flat (located on the south side of Syracuse) I loved to play school with my siblings. Being senior only to my two-year old sister (with my brother and two older sisters pulling rank), I was not often granted the role of teacher. But oh, when those rare moments presented themselves, I would organize our makeshift classroom and shuffle Dad's old Niagara Mohawk Power Corporation logoed papers to orchestrate the lesson. More times than not, my siblings would quit and wander off to another more exciting game or make-believe adventure before I could have the opportunity to collect the homework. I have learned that some things WILL never change. I also have learned that some things SHOULD never change. School should be as it was when I played on my porch as a child. It should be joyful, imaginative, fun, and motivational.

Journal entry: Mary Ellen – 3/2/1999

I dream of a future when education is personal, when learning is a valued journey, and when the individual is revered. I dream of a future that allows communities to grow in trust and harmony *because of* and *for* the children. If there were not an artificially imposed distinction between natural education and formal education, children would view the world as their classroom. Coexistence and behavioral norms would be developed in the living-learning environment called society, rather than in structured settings that emphasize strict conformity and behavioral compliance above all else.

Journal entry: Mary Ellen – 4/23/1999

We must reform the American Education System. What do we have to lose? Life as we know it? Our society is being attacked, attacked from within. Our enemy, increasing in power, is beginning to overwhelm us and undermine our hopes. Our enemy's name is Apathy.

Journal entry: Mary Ellen – 6/3/1999

Leonardo da Vinci would work through a problem towards a solution by putting it on the back burner of his mind. If I were to begin to sort through some of the complexities surrounding our educational dilemma, how would I begin sorting this out? I took the advice of Michael J. Gelb. He authored a book entitled, How to Think like Leonardo da Vinci, Seven Steps to Genius Every Day. He suggested that one develop 100 questions to ponder. This process is known as "the inspiration of curiosity, curiosito."

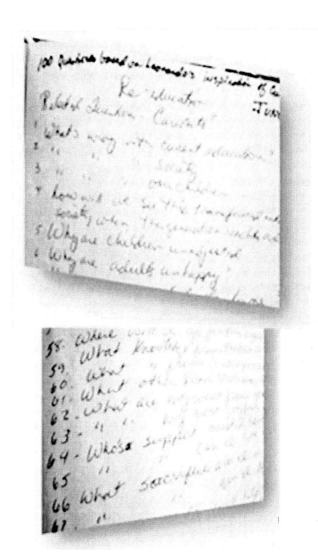

CHAPTER 2

On a picture perfect summer day ...

The Unexpected Prototype

"The Diversity Project"

"If we all did the things we are capable of, we would astound ourselves." **Thomas Edison**

Perspective: Mary Ellen

It was a picture perfect summer day in 2005 when we sat at the most beautiful outdoor café on the shores of Lake Ontario. We inhaled the gourmet aromas of portabella mushroom appetizers as our imaginations searched for a common theme to wrap around our educational intentions, sharing a unit of study.

It had been just a few months prior to this lovely day when a technology specialist, Kim, had come into my room and said, "Mary Ellen, have you got a minute? We are starting a video conference in the French room and I think you'd be interested in seeing this."

After my visit to Swaz's classroom, my head filled like warm water in a tub. My thoughts began to soak in all the possibilities that new technology brought to our doorstep. Fighting the natural instinct to dismiss the overwhelming anxiousness that change can bring, I allowed myself to compartmentalize just one change. I would make use of videoconferencing to continue the flow of water into the lukewarm tub of thought.

Kim is a very wise technology leader because she simply invited me to voice one hope (with no strings attached) of how I might like to use videoconferencing. My answer was to reinforce VTS (Visual Thinking Strategies), a technique whereby the viewers of visual media can begin to explore their perceptions. This visual literacy would soon be employed beyond our classroom by viewing pieces of art from collections at the Syracuse Everson Museum and the London Museum of Portraiture. My conversation with Kim ended with a few simple but hopeful intentions. Kim would research places for my art students to experience VTS. The French students would come along in order to learn more about the visual language and to enhance their visual documentation for French class. All of us would contemplate creating a unit of study that might allow for an integration of combined purposes.

The topic of our lunch meeting at Tin Pan Galley, Sackets Harbor, NY, was born. It was on that picturesque day that we had a convergence of positive intent for a better and more meaningful way to teach. This way would enable us to better prepare our students for the 21st century, by making purposeful use of present day technology. In so doing, we would set the bar for America.

"Diversity – diversité" – was the topic we chose to use to entice and engage our students as we embarked upon an educational journey. We did not know where it would lead. As we took our last sips of iced tea, we felt satisfied that we had outlined enough ideas to get us started. We had also built up enough courage and trust in our cause to move forward with conviction. Kim delivered the statement that would define our next year together. She stated, "We will be presenting this in San Diego a year from now at NECC (The National Educational Computing Conference)." Laughing at Kim's nonchalant attitude, we all paused. Our eyes darted back and forth around the table. Our next round of nervous laughter surfaced. Swaz and I acknowledged aloud, "She's not kidding!"

Diversity – the project
Beginning: the honeymoon

We each greeted our high school students with enthusiasm in our respective classrooms. We explained that the upcoming unit of study would be multidisciplinary. We added that the French and art classes would be combined and co-taught by both subject matter teachers.

We highlighted our goals of teaching each group VTS and movie making technology skills, while providing them with an avenue for voicing their views regarding diversity. Keeping in mind their interests, the art students were invited to focus on perspective and other art elements. The French students were encouraged to entertain the cultural dimensions of diversity while utilizing the French language in their projects.

The students seemed excited to try out a new format that would connect them to teams of fellow students from another class while enjoying the freedom to discuss, choose, and create a media project.

The middle – the honeymoon is over

After incorporating various teaming strategies to connect students interested in similar perspectives of diversity, the teams were then charged with the task of developing a plan and executing the creation of a five minute movie to be shared with one another. The students were advised of the possibility of sharing this information with a larger audience at some point in the future.

In phase one of teaming, everyone was on their best behavior. They behaved in similar fashion to how families might act when a guest has been invited to dinner. Students politely listened to one another while personalities and ideas rose to the surface like cream on butter. By the time the teams were moving from phase two to phase three (delegating jobs and starting production), the honeymoon was over. We began to hear grumblings of some students not pulling their weight. Complaints quickly turned into close-minded statements and inquiries such as, "What does this have to do with French or art anyway?"

We temporarily became disheartened as these statements reflected the very antithesis of our intent. We hoped to facilitate the opening of our students' minds and the broadening of their perspectives, while teaching them to celebrate individual differences as well as commonalities.

Phase four was time to present. It was clear by now which teams gelled well together and which teams endured difficulties, yet persevered. Finally, we acknowledged that there were teams that became unglued; thus, they were unable to complete their assigned tasks despite our best efforts to assist.

The presentations were not a disappointment! Students showed their work with great pride. They justified their choices with sound reasoning that was based on the melding of their research and experience. The final products were as diversified as their styles and topics. Some expressed diversity based on race and appearance. Others creatively pushed perceptions to their cultural limits through topics such as food, hairstyle, fashion, and religious beliefs. The students felt their accomplishments both as individuals and as collective members of classroom teams. We reflected upon our processes openly with the students and then challenged them to share their work with broader audiences. We welcomed one such opportunity. It was a building–wide assembly that was open to the community. We also requested our students' permission to present their work at professional presentations. We accepted the invitation from Dr. Jacquelyn Kibbey at the State University of New York at Oswego. We later presented to the local chapter of PDK (Phi Delta Kappa). Then, just as Kim had predicted, we traveled across America to San Diego and shared our project with a small group of 20 other interested professionals at the NECC Conference.

Perspective: Swaz

The advanced French students had been engaged in a videoconference with the Cleveland Museum of Art, taking part in a "Speak to Learn" activity to develop their vocabulary skills while viewing art pieces from the museum. As the spark of interdisciplinary projects was generated in the room, it triggered a powerful thought. Kim stated, "Art in a French classroom, Mary Ellen should see this!" She ran to the art room and dragged back an art teacher who would be amazed by the effect of videoconferencing, a powerful medium to connect professionals in a given field with students of a given academic area.

As students interacted within their groups and as the moderator in Cleveland conducted the game, many of the pieces of the diversity project began to unfold. There would be an art teacher and a French teacher, an interdisciplinary project on the subject of diversity, students working in teams producing bilingual movies on a topic of their choice, and technology as the means and tool to carry the voices of our students. Such were the pieces that, little by little, would create the amazing, colorful, diverse mosaic that would become "The Diversity Project."

The emergence of the Diversity Project came about quite naturally. There was little concern given to logistical impediments. Some art students were not taking French and some French students were not enrolled in art. We designed a project that would give all students an avenue for expressing and sharing their views beyond the confines of their classrooms. Our goal was to help students embrace diversity and produce powerful short films on issues of their choice. They delved into themes such as race, food, cultural differences, national origin, faith, economic and social status, etc. The students not only fulfilled the plan as conceptualized, but they also expanded the vision and produced little gems that we would proudly showcase for the whole school (in the context of an assembly), for the nation (at the NECC conference in San Diego), and for the world (via the internet and an online mega conference). Each team consisted of an art student, a French student, and a technologically astute student. Together, they utilized a computer program, Windows Movie Maker, to design movies that captured their views on the issue of diversity. For several weeks, our 5th period classes combined forces. Groups brainstormed ideas, wrote storyboards, and produced original films. Admittedly, there were some tough times when some students were unable to understand the meaning of this project and could not see the big picture. We knew, though, that education, in its tradition of compartmentalization, was the culprit. We defiantly plugged along, knowing that we were doing the right thing.

Once the films were completed, our closing activity was to conduct a videoconference with a group of young French students who were studying English in a technical school outside of Paris, France. This activity served as a way to work with first impressions and stereotyping. Once again, it showcased the beautiful diversity that surrounds us. We invited several panelists of varying professions, origins, genders, and ages to participate in the process. One of our guests was a female Franco-American singer who would perform for all of our high school students. We asked all panelists to introduce themselves to the students from France by only revealing their names. Then, the French students were encouraged to make guesses about the panelists based solely upon what they observed.   They were asked questions about the panelists' marital status, nationality, age, and profession. The large screen projection gave both groups the feeling that they were sitting across from one another even though they were an ocean away. We kept track of the students' answers on a big chart. As we expected, their perceptions were often far off the mark. In a subtle yet meaningful way, teachers and students reached beyond the confines of the classroom setting to bring closure to a project that had allowed all of us to reach far beyond our immediate walls. We showcased our differences and our commonalities in a manner that educated and inspired.

Word of the diversity project reached the professional community and we had the honor of presenting to the local chapter of PDK (Phi Delta Kappa) that spring.   Café Mira, a local restaurant with an amazing décor, high ceilings, and gourmet cuisine, had never seen so much equipment. We had screens, LCD projectors, laptop computers, speakers, and cords, cords, and more cords. We talked about our process and showcased sample films that our students had created. We ended our presentation with a live pastel drawing of a detail of Michelangelo's, "The Creation." The sketch was created by an awkward French teacher, who was desperately trying to stay within the lines; a tech coordinator, who held her own beautifully; and an art teacher who kept us all together and made sure that we did not accidentally create a completely new, surprising piece of art. This artistic creation unfolded to the beat of the Beatles' song, "Come Together," which was playing in the background. The song served as timekeeper since our art work was to be completed before the last note. Not surprisingly, Café Mira patrons requested that the sound be turned down, but our audience was impressed and we left the venue with a new energy and an undeniable sense that our team was *coming together* nicely.

World Class

Perspective: Mary Ellen

Before we knew it, we were invited to present to a class of upcoming teachers that were in Dr. Jacquelyn Kibbey's interdisciplinary course at the State University of New York at Oswego. Dr. Kibbey, a wonderful advocate for 21st century methods of teaching and learning, hosted us graciously. The session mirrored the presentation that we had made for the Phi Delta Kappa group with the inclusion of time for students to work in teams. This allowed students an opportunity to brain*stream** ways in which they could weave our methodologies into their content areas. First, we solicited general feedback and observations from the class of roughly 25 future art, English, health, math, science, and Spanish teachers. Although the response to our students' work was highly favorable, and attentiveness was at an all time high, we were amazed that these undergrads were already falling under the weight of the antiquated traditional views of education. They were viewing us as progressive, if not revolutionary. We were flabbergasted by their reactions. Some suggested that the diversity project might be feasibly undertaken by an art teacher or by students who were not required to take Regents exams. Others alluded to the time constraints of such a project. Some students felt as if they could not reasonably enter their new professions with such non-traditional methods. Other students seriously questioned the idea of collaborating with colleagues older than themselves. We were able to dispel their fears so that they could approach our methodologies from an energizing standpoint. After dissipating the fog of stereotypes, concerning who we are (ironically the whole point of our diversity project), we modeled what we preached by creatively challenging the class to think of possible opportunities to use the suggested methodology within their content areas. We then shifted the students into team building activities. After about 20 minutes, the groups reported back with wonderful ideas. They agreed that teaming, giving students more choices as well as providing interdisciplinary and presentation options, could enrich the educational experience for our Information Age students.

We had started our project in a school and were pleased to have moved on to the community and then on to a state university. As we heard that NECC (the National Educational Computing Conference) was holding its annual event in San Diego, CA, we set out to present there in July of 2006. Once our proposal was accepted, we tried to secure funding. Thanks to the support of PDK and our school district, we were heading to sunny California. This was by far the largest education conference any of us had ever attended. It was an honor to be a part of an organization that truly represents the future of our schools, our profession, and our students. Our presentation went without a glitch and one of the participants, a school administrator, was so impressed that she stayed in touch with us and arranged a videoconference that would allow her teachers, in rural Ohio, to learn about our process and engage in a dialogue with us.

We had sparked a level of excitement in our students that confirmed our intention of creating more authentic educational experiences. We had planted a seed in the minds of a handful of teachers, and in so doing, nourished an atmosphere of intrigue. From sunny Sackets Harbor to sunny San Diego, the diversity project had grown in ways that we had never imagined. Without knowing it, it was becoming the prototype for something much bigger, something that would reveal itself a year and a half later.

* As an alternative to brainstorming, *"brainstreaming"* allows for a true flow of ideas.

CHAPTER 3

It was an early morning breeze in September.

NCLB: No Child Left Behind?

No, ACT now:

ALL CHILDREN TREASURED!

"Think wrongly if you please, but in all cases, think for yourself."

Doris Lessing

Perspective: Mary Ellen – September 2008

There was an early morning breeze in September and a flock of geese flew over head in perfect formation. As I gazed upward looking out my classroom window, I marveled at the synchronization of form and rhythm that the flock maintained. All of the members were equally dispersed and if one lagged behind, the others compensated and adjusted so that no one was left behind. This cohesiveness was unlike what has happened with our country's educational policy. Despite the good intentions highlighted in its title, "No Child Left Behind", and of its intent to help all American children achieve preset standards and increased levels of educational accomplishments, the No Child Left Behind Act created an unforeseeable dilemma within our educational system. By creating standards and exemplars, the desired educational outcomes were being identified across the country. By narrowly defining educational progress through the tallying of test results only, we have completely missed the boat. The results have been disastrous! We are fooling ourselves into thinking that no child is actually left behind. Our educational boat has capsized. We need to provide life vests.

Journal entry: Mary Ellen – 1999
"Dead fish"

While discussing our views on the educational system, a former student of mine, Eliza, shared a symbolic story that involved her father, Jim. Jim and his friends had a hunting camp in the Adirondacks for years. One day the Department of Environmental Conservation showed up and began pulling trout upon trout out of the nearby lake. Jim, coming upon the D.E.C. researchers and seeing a pile of dead trout on the shoreline, asked, "What are you doing with all of our trout?" The D.E.C. researchers went on to give a lengthy explanation about the acidity in the water and the various reasons why it got that way. The D.E.C. researchers continued to explain that, to their astonishment, this lake, unlike the others nearby, was full of trout. They explained that other lakes had been depleted. The research leaders were catching as many trout as possible but for a good reason. They explained that they were investigating in order to discover the reasons for the fish's survival. This way, they reasoned, they might be able to save the fish in the other waters. To that Jim replied, "I know why we have trout here." "You do?" the D.E.C. researcher said with great interest. "Yes," said Jim, "because my friends and I put lime in the water every year to combat the acidity so that our trout can flourish." "Oh!" responded the D.E.C. research leader. The moral of the story? Why not ask those already present what they know, think, and recommend, before you start poking at all of the defenseless fish. Another moral of the story? Stop killing more fish while you try to figure out what makes them thrive.

Journal entry: Mary Ellen
"Dead in the water" kids

Note: to protect identities, personal information, including names and titles, have been modified. Course names used are arbitrary.

Two weeks ago, during parent-teacher conferences, only two sets of parents came to see me. Then surprisingly, two teachers, Mr. Pompous and Ms. Archaic came to see me about the same two students, Will and Chad. Will has been my art student since 9th grade. He is now a pseudo-senior. Chad is a pseudo-junior. They are in a place similar to limbo, not quite on grade level. I have taught art to Chad since his freshman year. I've known him for four years now, one of which was only through visiting him in an institution. A third student, Brianna, will be presented in this section as well.

"Fish out of water"

Will

"Will is not cutting it," said Mr. Pompous in an aggressive tone. "I'm coming to you as if you were his coach." Without much of a breath in between, he went on to say, "I just spoke with his mother who has just seen the science teacher whose class Will is doing nothing for either." Then taking another breath for air, "It seems he only wants to do his art and music." Mr. Pompous's pace, intensity, and volume of speech now increasing, he added, "Well, if I'm being held accountable and my name is being printed in the paper with our test results and Will isn't cutting it, then I'm going to let you know, guidance know, the principal know, and his mother know that he should drop. If all he wants to do is his art and music, he should drop school altogether and do that!" The voice of Mr. Pompous had reached a momentum that I dared not attempt to interrupt. As I watched the conviction and fervor that was being expended to fight and conquer that which threatened the "good teacher's" reputation, I saw the sad truth. This teacher, as has been the case with many educators, has been conditioned by the system's mandates, which promote pseudo-accountability at the expense of educating our children. The system has perpetuated a prideful and protectionist approach to meeting the standards. Pride can become destructive. Pride often prevails over the truth of our jobs as teachers and parents. Our most important calling is to watch over and guide our children toward their own success, not a pseudo-success defined by a test, the system, or the state.

My memory flashed back to Will in 9th grade. He was meek and withdrawn, yet very witty. He excelled in art creation and failed to submit any required written work.

The day after the conferences, Will and I had a conversation. He showed me his full notebook! "Why haven't you handed any of this in?" I asked. He replied, "Because it is not in any format that you want. I can't do that. I just write my thoughts, poems, and feelings down, but they are just there, all sort of jumbled together." Tears came to his eyes and then streams of frustration and shame rolled down his cheeks. The following day, I explained to Mr. Pompous that I had more insight into Will's situation. I asked him if he was aware of Will's medically diagnosed chemical imbalance.   He retorted, "FOR CRYING OUT LOUD, MOST OF US HAVE A CHEMICAL IMBALANCE. THAT'S NO EXCUSE!" I think my body leaned back at a 45 degree angle.   As I breathed more deeply, I felt my calm still in charge. I went on to share details of the conversation I had had with Will. I told Mr. Pompous how Will had been working diligently to finish preparing his oil painting for an upcoming, opening reception and exhibit at a local restaurant.   I wanted him to realize that this was quite an accomplishment and an honor. I explained that Will, however, was behind in all of his written work for me as well. I made another attempt to appeal to Mr. Pompous's emotional   intelligence.   I   revealed   that   Will admitted, just the day before, that he was capable of doing the required work. Will explained that when he sat down to do the work, too many thoughts came   at   once,   and   so   he   gave   up.   "THAT'S BULLSHIT!" Mr. Pompous's words were like darts that hit me squarely between the eyes. "I gave him ways to organize, I taught him to break down the components," he fumed. I understood that Mr. Pompous's frustration was because he did not see any effort from Will. I then mentioned that I had scheduled an appointment with Will's mother, and I went on to remark that I had a conversation with Will about *all* of his classes and that we agreed to try setting up a time for him to work with me as his *focus tutor*.

The next day, Will reported to his tutoring session during his lunch as planned. The following day brought the news that Will had gone to the guidance office to check up on his schedule, graduation requirements, and also to inquire about dropping his current Spanish class in exchange for an easier course. He was told by his Spanish teacher that he neither demonstrated any effort, nor sought any help. Understandably, his Spanish teacher was befuddled. That day, during his lunch-work, I confronted Will again. "I'd rather help you get to this overdue work, but we need to address your lack of effort. Tell me what your intentions are, for education here and for your future." With his head bowed down and while biting his lower lip, he softly mumbled the details about his visit to guidance. He shared, "I won't be able to graduate this year, even if I pass everything. I still need three more courses in addition to..." He shook his head in discouragement. "They say I'll even need one more gym credit. I'm confused. I thought I had four years of gym. I haven't ever failed gym." He continued without pausing. "In social studies class yesterday, the teacher told me [Will choked on his words], he told me I should drop, because I can't make it. He can't do that, he can't make me drop. I have the right to try [Will began to cry]. I have the right to fail on my own!" It is obvious that his teachers were not the only ones reaching a high level of frustration. I calmly but firmly told Will, "You can choose to do this or not, but it is not up to anyone else but you." His eyes lifted and I could see that Will was not finished with his education yet.

Will graduated the following year with a beautiful art exhibit under his belt. At the opening reception, the school superintendent came as one of the honored guests.

Flash forward to a decade later:

Several years later, my husband and I sat out on the deck of a lovely restaurant in Sackets Harbor, NY. We were enjoying a sunset dinner as we looked out over the shimmering waters of the harbor. Complimenting the ambiance and delicious food was the eclectic guitar playing that drew applause from the modest audience. Yes, it was Will. He was happily, fruitfully, and joyfully sharing the intellectual mastery of his guitar playing while singing with a deep, soulful voice. I chuckled to myself as I watched him gleefully thumb through his full and organized notebook of song selections.

Interestingly, there were four other teachers that we knew in the audience. I wondered if they gave any thought to how Will performed on his Regents exams. I suspect that, like us, their realm of appreciation was broadened by the sweet sounds of success and enriched by the positive spirit that brought forth such joy and harmony.

Chad

I was ushered through a brief security check before I was allowed to visit. I stated, "I'm his teacher. I just want to check in with him to see how he's doing." The staff member inquired, "Do you have anything with you that is sharp?" "No," I replied. The staff member stated, "Alright, come this way. You can visit him here. I will go get him."

I had heard that my student had a breakdown of sorts at school. He stood out as a real rebel, complete with the latest 22mm earplug and earlobe stretching tapers that made him look all the wilder. He had porcelain skin that sometimes took on a slight blue-green tint, especially on days when he seemed a bit dehydrated. His very blond hair was regularly shaved into a variety of shapes that easily absorbed the color of the week. His eyes were wide and soft and seemed to deepen during regular conversation. He entered the room, and I noticed that I was a bit shaky and nervous about seeing him. Embarrassed and hoping I wasn't violating his privacy, I was relieved that he agreed to see me. He quietly sat in a chair about three feet from mine and a faint smile dared to sneak onto his face. I began by thanking him and apologizing for my boldness to visit him at the hospital. I softly asked how he was, and he said, in an almost inaudible voice, "Fine." Not knowing what to do in our silence, I rambled on about courage, his talent, my prayers for him, and his friends missing him at school. He appreciated my good intentions and shared his feelings. He simply couldn't take the pressure anymore. He missed his dead mother. He loved his brother but not the responsibility of caring for him 24/7. He had many difficult days and the built-up weight deluded him into thinking that he might be better off dead. I listened attentively as security walked by in this psychiatric institution and my heart broke. I offered him my support, my faith, my great-aunt Gen-Gen's rosary beads and my prayers. It was a few weeks later that my rebel artist, wide-eyed and soft-smiling, returned with a hug and new art waiting to be expressed! With a chuckle, he reported to me that Aunt Gen-Gen's gift was confiscated as her rosary was considered to be a dangerous object. Feeling naïve and stupid, I offered thanks in my heart that he had given himself a second chance.

Today, fifteen years later, this young man, whose saving grace was his pure heart and his art, is now a successful entrepreneur and musician. He owns his own home and is a proud and responsible single parent and lover of life!

Brianna

Brianna is a naturally intelligent and inquisitive student. She's the only student out of fifty that, during a Sunday school lecture, called out to give her assessment on what constitutes a profession versus a vocation.

Brianna's approach in the art room, to create a self-portrait, lies within the realm of the fauves as she unknowingly gives the viewer a peek into her mind. She paints her eyes red, her nose orange, her cheeks and jaw purple, and her forehead yellow. Her composition fills the page and her face tilts down slightly with her eyes looking straight ahead, straight at you!

Brianna is just returning to school after three days of suspension. Her offense was repeatedly skipping detention. She was assigned detention for committing various infractions, including not doing her work. I asked Brianna about her situation. The exchange proceeded as follows:

Q: Brianna, why don't you do your school work?

A: I don't like it. It doesn't matter to me.

Q: What do you want out of life?

A: I want to be able to support myself.

Q: How do you plan to do that?

A: I need my high school diploma. I know that if I can't discipline myself enough to graduate, then no employer will want to hire me. They will think I'm not responsible.

Q: Why did you miss detention?

A: I didn't mean to skip. I didn't know I had detention until my brother called to tell me.

Q. Can you see the writing on the wall?

A. Yeah, well my mom and dad will probably move south and leave me the house. I'll need to get a job to pay for gas, taxes, food, and other stuff. I'll be able to find something.

Conclusion

If you are thinking that Will, Chad, and Brianna are three, out of several fish, who are attempting to swim upstream against a strong educational current, you are correct. At times, we as teachers, undermine students' efforts because we have neither asked nor listened. We have not led them through troubled waters. Instead, we have thrown them into the acidic waters of No Child Left Behind and its mandates. Although data will show that the majority of students (those who make it that far without dropping out or being forced to drop) pass the Regents exams, this number does not accurately capture the pain and injustices endured by those with special needs or those who are dominantly right-brained. Finally, Regents exams, while good for measuring the mastery of subject matter information, do little to assess other types of mastery. We miss the boat when we fail to emphasize and measure acquired knowledge and associative thinking skills as well as our students' ability to assimilate and problem solve. Our over-reliance on formalized testing has diminished the sense of empowerment that is created when students and teachers become unique and vital contributors to the educational process.

We as educators should strive to provide our fish with safe, healthy, and balanced waters. Teachers should handle children as fishermen would delicately handle fish that are too small or "not in season". Lure, catch, admire, and release them unharmed. Return them to the waters whereby they can thrive.

There is a world of problems to be solved and the answers won't be found in the state exams.

Perspective regarding state tests: Swaz

For 20 years, I helped to develop French tests at the state level. For 20 years, I took part in the writing and careful editing of every sentence of the tests I reviewed. Colleagues from different parts of the state and I discussed the placement of numerous punctuation marks as well as the addition and deletion of many words, phrases, and sentences. We questioned the level of difficulty of the passages, wondered if a given theme had its relevance in a particular test, and argued about word order, spelling, and syntax. Every year, after much toiling, we created a final product that we found to be fair, relevant to the targeted age group, and consistent with the identified mastery levels. We, as top educators in our fields, were proud of this chiseled, polished creation. Many of us had contributed to the final product. Still, I have grown somewhat opposed to systematic, standardized testing, to the extent that standardized testing reduces all students to one style of learning. Educators can undermine the potential of many students when they allow the content to be watered-down in order to assure that a greater number of students receive passing grades on their exams. In addition, I find testing that favors one learning style over another to be contrary to what we know about this 21st century generation. The 21st century learner strives to personalize, create, and individualize. Our students would be better served if we were to branch away from the use of one form of standardized testing to use other formats that equally complement other learning styles. Portfolio assessment, once deemed to be an in vogue and innovative assessment tool, is one such branch. We need to nurture and grow this assessment tree until all learning styles have a branch to call their own. As long as assessment tools adequately measure the degree to which pupils have achieved mastery of the standards set by our educational systems, they should be considered valuable.

Many administrators and educators believe that if we decrease our over-reliance on standardized testing, then we risk compromising a mechanism that is widely utilized to evaluate the competency of our teachers. Teacher accountability is very important and may also benefit from different measurement tools that take into consideration different teaching approaches and styles. When one asks how one can measure the mastery level of our teachers and students, we should respond by saying that we need to develop better tools that take into account the special and unique aspects of how these people function as educators and learners. We are no longer in a one size fits all world. It is agreed that we must make sure that clear mandates are in place and that teachers are held accountable while helping their students reach the proper level of understanding and subject matter mastery. Unlike state tests, the state and national *standards* allow for a much broader understanding of what constitutes learning. Testing procedures and teacher accountability should be more closely aligned with these established educational standards.

World Class

If we are indeed committed to preparing our students for the world and for the future, then we must be able to work cooperatively with our colleagues to create curriculum that generates meaningful connections. We must integrate differing but complementary subject areas and make use of technological tools as a means to enhance student experiences in the classroom and beyond. "If it's not broken, don't fix it." It IS broken, and we must work together as educators to fix it. We may meet much resistance from those who are accustomed to the status quo, but we must move forward for the greater good. My fellow teachers and I must come to understand that it is not all about us. A new generation is ready for learning and creating. If we were to refocus the energies that we currently expend on "teaching to the test" toward teaching students on their own terms, we would be well on our way to revolutionizing our current educational system.

"It's about truth, the real truth, not about analyzing data and interpreting it in your own way for your own reasons."   Françoise Piron

CHAPTER 4

As the colored
leaves floated
to the ground,
they mixed brilliantly
and naturally.

It's not all about us

"We have become not a melting pot but a beautiful mosaic. Different people, different beliefs, different yearnings, different hopes, different dreams."
Jimmy Carter

Perspective: Swaz

For far too long, the U.S. has adopted an ethnocentric attitude. This attitude has been perpetuated by the media. Many believe that this attitude is unfair, unhealthy, and obsolete. In an era of globalization, each country contributes to the world's tapestry. America is not the center of the world. Just as we have strengths and weaknesses as individuals, countries have various cultural models, all of which must be respected and valued. As members of the human race, we have much in common. There is too much criticism, too much lack of comprehension, and too much ignorance when it comes to valuing different individuals and nations. As our colleague Bill Jones (a professor in Legal Studies at the State University of New York at Canton) told us one day while we were discussing the implementation of our new course, "Here, in the U.S., you can be "un-American" when you're not a good citizen. What other country says that? You're never 'un-French' or 'un-British'." We agree with Professor Jones. It is time for our students to truly understand that we are all equal. We are citizens of the world, who are intricately connected to all human beings. No one country or culture is better than another. The flattening of the world has made it abundantly clear that it is not so much where you are that matters but what you know and what you can do with that knowledge.

Now, more than ever during these troubled times, it is essential to infuse our educational approach with global notions. Nationalistic sentiments around the world are on the rise. Xenophobia is becoming more prevalent. In hard times, people have the tendency to focus on their own needs and to blame the foreigners and/or the immigrants for taking their jobs or for causing ills to permeate society. Our students must learn to research, comprehend, and analyze the big picture so that they may become better equipped to integrate and meld into the world in a meaningful and productive way. They must develop their own educated understanding, which is free from preconceived notions, stereotypes, and/or falsehoods.

"If we are to achieve a richer culture, rich in contrasting values, we must recognize the whole gamut of human potentialities, and so weave a less arbitrary social fabric, one in which each diverse human gift will find a fitting place."   *Margaret Mead*

A personal story – Swaz
FRAN-WHAT?

One day I went to a local business where I had to provide my first name. Upon saying "Françoise", a very common name in the French-speaking world, the employee said, "Wow, your mom must not have liked you." This statement, although based on ignorance, was very offensive to me. The author of that line indirectly insulted my mother (who has always loved me), my father (who was just as responsible for choosing my first name), non-English speakers (whose names may be different, yet beautiful) and myself. Think of how much your name represents you. Remember, our students are often affronted when we misspell or mispronounce their names.

I tell this story to remind educators that a primary concern with regard to helping our students to become better "citizens of the world" is to develop a certain cultural and social sensitivity. We want students to meet people of different origins, to connect with them, and to embrace not only similarities but differences as well. We want them to be comfortable with Toufic from Lebanon, Wen from China and Yngvi from Iceland. We want them to welcome the unfamiliar with open hearts and arms.

Excerpts from Honor Society Induction speech: Swaz - November 2007

"I was born and raised in Switzerland. When I think of education in Europe, I think of a culture where academics prevail and where knowledge is the foundation of basic education. Philosophy, as a subject area, is valued, and all high school students have to take at least two years of philosophy. The great thing about this subject matter is that it teaches one why one thinks, how to think, and how to look at concepts and issues using multiple perspectives. Even without further formal education in philosophy, one has the intellectual discipline to do great things. Use it to innovate, to create, and to extrapolate. Think outside the box. Nurture the left side and the right side of your brain.

When I look back at my high school career, I remember absorbing many facts, retaining few, but learning how to think.

Math wasn't my strongest subject in high school, but when I went to university, I recall longing for the very structured mindset of algebra. In Switzerland, one immediately specializes in one major and two minors. I specialized in languages and literature. These formative high school years of education shape our minds as well as our futures. In his book, <u>The World is Flat</u>, Thomas Friedman makes the case that, in the current years of globalization and the development of information technology, it is more important to learn *how* to learn than to absorb information.

Consider this. Eight out of ten current kindergartners will one day have a job that has yet to be created.

World Class

Be passionate about what you love, love to learn, take classes that inspire you, look at the big picture, make connections and consider different perspectives. As you develop your minds, think with your hearts too. Stick up for what is right, even though that may not be the most popular viewpoint. As St. Exupéry wrote in his most famous children's book, <u>Le Petit Prince</u>, « On ne voit bien qu'avec le coeur. L'essentiel est invisible pour les yeux. » "It is only with the heart that one can truly see; what is essential is invisible to the eye." Trust your instincts, look beyond your immediate surroundings, and learn about the world. It is ready for you."

We now understand that we must open our hearts and minds to the world. These are examples of 10 cultural words to the wise.
Paraphrased from: http://findarticles. com/p/articles/mi_m0IBP/is_2_50/ai_n26828851/

1. In the U.S., it is the norm to outwardly display emotion towards loved ones, but public displays of

affection are considered disrespectful to people in Arab and Afghani cultures. Inquiring about a female member of the family is also frowned upon.

2. The OK symbol done with your fingers may be interpreted as *alright* for Americans, but it suggests the idea of worthlessness in France (like zero), money in Japan, and a part of the body in Brazil, Germany, and Russia.

3. Bringing gifts to a host/ hostess can be tricky. In France, bringing a bottle of wine is insulting because it suggests that their wine is not good enough. Bringing chrysanthemums is of very bad taste because those flowers are reserved for funerals. In Chinese cultures, at weddings, it is very auspicious to give a gift in pairs or to give an even amount of money. The number six is considered lucky and the number eight symbolizes wealth. Giving gifts in even numbers symbolizes good wishes to the new couple and the hope that they would stay together and live happily forever. Offering a clock is inappropriate. The Chinese word for clock is "zhong." It has the same pronunciation as the word for "the end." Also, the

phrase "to give a clock" phonetically sounds the same as "to send to [their] end."

4. Korean culture may find it insulting or even aggressive when a person with whom they are having a conversation looks directly into their eyes. The most polite way to talk to them may be to avoid eye contact altogether.

5. In the Middle East, the left hand is used for bodily hygiene, so reserve your right hand for eating.

6. In Nepal, Hindu temples are off-limits to foreigners and should not be photographed without permission.

7. In some Korean and Arabic cultures, elders are honored in such a manner that they should be addressed and served first. Others should stand when an older person enters the room.

8. Pointing with the finger is the most universally offensive gesture. In most cultures, outside of the United States, it is much more appropriate to point with a closed hand or with a gesture of the head. Many cultures consider the pointing finger as rude or obscene.

9. In the Arabic world, it is considered extremely rude to put your feet up in such a way as to expose the soles of the shoes. It is viewed as highly unclean and offensive.

10. Blowing your nose in public is seen as coarse and impolite in many cultures. It would be appropriate to discreetly leave the room before doing so.

CHAPTER 5

The leaves covered
the ground,
limbs now fully
exposed.

*The state of the
classroom*

"Our controlled frenzy creates the illusion of a well-ordered existence.   We move from crisis to crisis, responding to the urgent and neglecting the essential."   Brennan Manning

Journal entry: Mary Ellen - Sept. 26, 2000

His name is posted on the morning news. Accident-died at 12:30 am. "What? What?" I gasp. "Oh, honey, did you know him?" asks my husband. "What?" I say in disbelief. It starts to hit me. "Not him, not him! What did they say?"

I am sputtering now and my volume increases. "What? What? Did he die?" The words spewing out of my mouth begin to reach my brain. My husband, now holding me, says, "Honey, I'm so sorry, I wouldn't have let you see it like that had I known it was one of your students. I'm sorry." Mark cannot shelter me from this. Still I soak in the warmth of his arms. I realize once again, how fragile life is. I say a prayer for my student's family.

The ride to work is the only time to release my emotion regarding the shocking news before I need to be strong for others. I put Sarah McLachlan into my CD player and crank it to drown myself out.

In school, I cannot hold back my tears. My eyes moisten with tears as I enter the building. Alone in the hallway, on the way to my room, I hear myself weeping softly. Outside my door, after the bell rings, I watch students pass by in a parade of

shock, silence, and tears. Down the hall, a boy
leans against his locker. Then, he retreats into the
study hall as his grief chokes past his attempt to
contain it.

The announcement instructs us to go to
class meetings. The entire student body moves
through the halls in a sea of silence, ABSOLUTE
SILENCE! The sound of it strikes my aching heart
with profoundness. It is deafening! Suddenly we are
all one: teachers, students, test givers, test takers,
administrators, support staff, and disciplinarians.
Inside the cafeteria, with the ninth grade class, I
witness what our small community is all about.
Literally, every child is grieving, if not for him, for
the pain of each other and for the loss of one of
their own, a fellow youth. All day we repeat the
same actions with a wide variety of students. We
give a hug and ask, "How are you doing?" We hear
cries and offer words of comfort. Soft-spoken
students float through the halls for the first two
periods. Many are seen in clusters of huddled
friends simply making laps around our corridors.

Being a teacher is so much more important than one can imagine. The responsibilities associated with this profession are real and fiercely urgent! During our time of mourning as well as for years to come, many of us would wonder what we could have done or said that would have made a difference for this one precious child.

Journal entry: Mary Ellen - April 2, 2008

I reflect upon my journal entries of over a decade ago, anticipating a revolution in education or a "civil war". Colin Powell, Secretary of State under President George W. Bush, was on the news last night discussing our national security and how it is based on the success of education. He mentioned that our country is weakening against the power of China and India. Here we go. Prepare the troops. This war, before affecting our nation at large will first see the suffering from personal battles. Civil wars fought within the walls of our schools will scar and divide us. But fight we must as the struggle will be worth it. We must keep our eyes on the prize. No, not for American superiority but, rather, for global tolerance, harmony, and concern for the quality of life of all mankind.

As Powell said, "It is a case of national security." How can we achieve a safe national environment when we cannot ensure personal security? Let us keep in mind that every student is a precious source of potential and hope for the future. Schools have awesome responsibilities. May we holistically nurture and care for every child, so that we don't needlessly lose another precious life.

Journal entry: Mary Ellen - March 11, 2009

"I just heard that there was a loaded rifle found in the backseat of a kid's car," she whispered. She continued, "There was some little fender bender in the parking lot and the trooper was there. While investigating, he found that the gun was loaded! The shell was right in the chamber!"

The rest of the school day unfolded while the limbs of the trees bravely faced the cruel north winds. The students entered class and got out their supplies.   One art easel remained obtrusively empty, waiting for its artist. He never came. As the canvas patiently donned only three layers of color, barely enough to cover its pure, white, textured skin, the rest of the students and the teacher pretended to be normal.

"Where's Paul?" I asked.

"I think he's in trouble," replied his classmate, as her large brown eyes innocently looked up from her multi-colored palette. "I think he's in BIG trouble," she added.

The student went on to explain the circumstances that surrounded her friend's problems. Her heart was breaking for him, for his poor choices, and for his loss of more innocence. On some level, although we were still in shock, we already knew how grateful we were for the God-incidence, the fender-bender.

World Class

Perspective: Mary Ellen

Schools are under tremendous pressure. As microcosms of society, we often need police protection to maintain safety. We practice "lock out drills" for potential harm that can come from without and "lockdown drills" for harm that can come from within. Teachers, administrators, and every staff member face new responsibilities on a daily basis. They must have heightened awareness of students' conversations as well as any signs of potential violence through writings, actions, computer use, and any other form of expression. We are on the front lines daily for our entire careers. We need the prayers as well as the love and support of our communities and our government in a manner consistent with the support that we proudly offer to our military troops, through funding, good military bases, recruitment of soldiers, and excellent training. Support for our educational system is a matter of national security as well.

Journal entry: Mary Ellen - March 2008
Sabotage and the pecking order

Prior to initiating our new course, our administration wisely called a meeting of school leaders. I believe the strategy was in part to create professional transparency in hopes of moving forward in a harmonious way. Most conflicts are initiated through the perception that one's territory is being threatened. To guard against this perception would be of utmost importance as we moved forward. One afternoon, we were given a chance to explain our intentions and to describe our new course. Our hope was to bring our most diverse, professional representatives to the table to generate some ideas and to entertain some questions. We hoped that this would help the Media Literacy Class to get off on the right foot. In attendance were our superintendent, principal, assistant principal, guidance counselors, athletic director, and technology leader. Our library specialist and union president were invited; however, they were unable to attend. The meeting went well and some good ideas were generated. My favorite idea was that the class might be housed in the auditorium. The auditorium is a universal space that could easily accommodate teaming and student/community presentations. All present seemed to be relieved that the state regulation 100.5(d) recognized media literacy for credit under the Art Department. This fact allowed us to proceed without fear of posing a threat to other content area teachers. The group was cautiously supportive of the requested two period block of time allotted for the class as well as the designated space and technological resources necessary to kick off this 21st century course.

Word soon traveled that we were approved to begin our new course in the fall. It did not take long for the opposition to engage in covert actions to undermine the class before it was ever formerly announced. The pecking order became immediately defined by those who wished to undermine the new course offering. Worse yet, my eyes were opened to the gross prejudice that is cast upon the students. One professional stopped me to say that she had heard that I was planning to offer a new course and that she was very interested in learning more about it. I naïvely responded that I had just drafted my course description and that I had sample units that I would be happy to share. Her response was a tacit acceptance to read my work. She then quickly added, "I hope you realize that there will be a ripple effect because you will need the use of technology. Furthermore, I want to let you know that if I have the choice between a student from a core class using a computer or an art student using one, there is no way that a core class student would not have access to a computer when s/he needed it." I was sickened by the illustration of how this type of judgmental attitude defines our students' pecking order in the eyes of some professionals. Sadly, this discrimination is rampant within our system. It is seen in many different arenas. Opposition is created in academics, arts, athletics, life skills, special needs, technology, etc. Let's not underestimate the destructive force of the contrived pecking order that exists in our schools. Teachers are devalued but the damage done to the self-image of students at the lower end of the pecking order can have devastating results. When students' strengths lie within the less favored curriculum areas, they often learn that they do not enjoy the same respect, consideration, or favors afforded to others. This twisted hierarchy in our school systems limits the potential growth and success of our teachers and students alike. For too long, the status quo, like other forms of discrimination, has been tolerated. True academic potential will be realized when this disparaging inequity is exposed and dealt with accordingly. A second, more disturbing attempt to sabotage the birth of our course came in the form of a colleague's covert complaints to our principal and teachers' union president. This colleague (who had limited knowledge about the course), upon hearing of it, tried to convince the principal that proper procedure was not being followed and that this was a violation of guidelines. Not satisfied by the positive stance that the principal maintained, the colleague attempted to garner support from the union president. Thankfully, the union president (objectively fair and well-versed in protocol and contract agreements) responded by asking the disgruntled peer if s/he would expect to have the art teacher's permission to run a new course in his/her area of expertise. This battle ended. I remain befuddled as to why this colleague was so threatened by the course that it became a personal mission to undermine its success. What made this course a threat? Perhaps this episode indicated that we were, in fact, causing a crack in the barricades created by this nearly insurmountable wall. We were fighting to create change rather than maintain the norm. Yes, everything changes. That we can count on. As we sing out our mantra, "IT IS ALL CONNECTED," rest assured, the personal changes created from this battle will have lasting and significant ripple effects.

If our country's security depends on our collective efforts to improve education, then our world's security depends on the same. It is worth the fight.

World Class

LET'S PONDER – Thoughts from Swaz

- Most current educational models were developed during the 19th century (Industrial Revolution) and the 20th century (Electric and Electronic Revolution).
- Many methods of the past are now OBSOLETE.
- The world has become much flatter, ask Thomas Friedman. (Friedman, Thomas (2005), The World is Flat, by Farrar, Straus & Giroux, New York)
- It is not so much where you live that matters but what you can do.
- Asian workers can do the same work as Americans for a fraction of the cost.
- Computers can do the same left-brained work as humans but for a fraction of the cost, at a much faster pace, and with a higher degree of accuracy; ask Daniel Pink (Pink, Daniel H. (2006), A Whole New Mind, Penguin Group, Inc., New York.)
- It is time for us to realize that paradigms have shifted.

- The internet is causing ideas to spread exponentially.

- Our current students are digital natives. They think and function differently than students of the past.

- Our current students' future jobs do not yet exist.

- Give students a chance to express themselves with the tools they are most comfortable using.

- Help students develop their brains so that they can help this country stay competitive in a global world.

- During the oil crisis of the seventies in France, the following slogan became popular: « Nous, on n'a pas de pétrole, mais on a des idées! » "We don't have oil but we have ideas." It is time to rehabilitate this slogan and apply it to our modern, technologically advanced society.

- Let's give our students the chance to develop the most critical skills to help them succeed professionally and personally. Let's encourage and teach problem solving, collaboration, leadership, adaptability, initiative, effective communication, accessing and analyzing information, etc.

- May our students learn to think and work smarter not harder. This will not happen solely by listening to lectures and taking notes from an overhead projector.

- Technology is an integral part of this educational revolution. It reaches far beyond the use of computers. Technology must become a cultural component of our revolution by making use of multimedia in powerful and meaningful ways. It will make its operators better people and the world a better place.

- Educators must break free from the traditional teaching approaches and embrace the use of technology as a tool of truth, not just mere convenience.

Our world's greatest resource is the human spirit. Coupled with genetic and cultural-generational wisdom, we have what it takes to make profound changes. Our country's greatest resource is our American ingenuity. In the 1800s, our country had just embarked upon an age known as the Industrial Revolution. Our schools were designed to prepare students for production lines and mechanized labor. We are currently at a similarly pivotal moment in our history. May we fearlessly move forward and give our students the best tools to succeed in this 21st century world.

CAN YOU SAY OBSOLETE?

Our current educational model was established decades ago when the world was much smaller and less connected. Many aspects of the current educational model are no longer valid. Current students' brains may even be wired differently than those of their parents, the baby boomers. We are doing our children a significant disservice by continuing to push them through an archaic system that does not fully meet their educational needs. No wonder the high school dropout rate has continued to climb. Our learners need new stimuli that must be customized for each learning style and personality. The educational

model that we will present in the next few chapters takes into consideration our current clientele, the tools that we have at our disposal, and the issues that we all want to address to make our world a better place. It focuses on collaboration while allowing students to work at their own pace. It encourages teams to capitalize on the strengths of its members while supporting expression and creativity. Teachers are facilitators of learning. They model what they preach by working in teams. Learners, and teachers alike, divide tasks based on each other's strengths. They guide one another through the learning process in a way that entices all to be invested in the process.

CHAPTER 6

As the ice formed on the shore, one layer at a time...

The layout of the course – all the pieces are coming together

"Give a man a fish, you feed him for a day.   Teach a man to fish, you feed him for a lifetime."
Chinese Proverb

Perspective: Mary Ellen

We have arrived at the threshold where apathy meets our desire to be heard and understood. It becomes more difficult for both student and teacher to mask the intrinsic need to explore and express that which interests them. From years of conditioning, many of us have forgotten that we still have freedom within the mandates of state and national standards. The dropout rates steadily increase while our measurement of success is overly dependent upon test scores.

Like cold, blue–grey ice mounds that develop imperceptibly on the surface of the lake, our attempts to peel back the crusted layers of apathy are strategically chiseled away by giving our students more choice and a voice.

Our design to reengage students in a more authentic way incorporates ongoing opportunities for students and teachers to make individual and collaborative choices. The outcome of students' work, we hope, will result in an expression that reflects their contribution. In the context of media literacy as our content area, it is truly the learning process that takes precedence in the design. The intent of the curriculum is to break apathy's hold on our youth while educating the Net Geners about the very medium that governs their daily existence, the media. The prospect of what it might look like in a classroom, to truly give students a voice and choice, is intimidating, and even threatening, as it relates to the well-ingrained role as "the teacher in control of his/her class." It will require us, as teachers, to do something very risky and frightening at the same time, to LET GO!

Journal entry: Mary Ellen - May 2004

I am excited to be on a spiritual retreat up here in Wadhams Hall, Ogdensburg, NY. The anticipated rest and soulful nourishment that I yearn for will surely come in this serene and sacred setting. The priest addresses the crowd of 70 in the chapel. After an opening prayer, that is like a soothing balm on my tired mind, I settle in to listen to the priest's lecture (adapted from Sister

Sebastia's story, "Catching Monkeys", as told in <u>Stories They Will Remember</u> by Rose D. Sloat, Darryl S. Doane, p. 64). The story goes something like this:

There was a cute little monkey who joyfully lived in the jungle. He would play and explore all day and gather his food from nature. One day, the monkey, leaping from tree to tree, caught sight of a luscious banana that lay neatly tucked inside a hole of the tree's trunk. As the monkey gleefully fit his tiny and supple hand into the hole to grab the banana, he was unaware that this was a trap set to keep him in captivity.

Still, blissfully anticipating the rich taste of this delicacy, the monkey attempted to pull the banana out of the tree's trunk. He found that he was stuck. At first, the monkey calmly tried to maneuver the banana and his hand free but as each attempt rendered him unsuccessful, he became more and more frantic. Soon, the monkey was squealing and crying. The harder he tried to free himself, the more he cried aloud. A wise and kind person happened along during a walk through the jungle. Upon hearing the distressed monkey, he stopped at the base of the tree. This person possessed many, many years of life and he had great gifts of observation. He, therefore, was a very wise person, indeed. The monkey, now crying and screaming loudly and uncontrollably, did not notice the wise person. Having observed this behavior before, and knowing that monkeys were trapped by placing banana bait inside the hole, the wise man called out to the little monkey, "LET GO"!

Surely, I embellished the parable to emphasize that which mattered most to me. Of all the experiences I had at that retreat, many profound, the story of the monkey and the banana hit my heart in a special way. In reflection, I came to realize that if I wanted to enjoy the luscious rewards of watching students engaging in their education in a new and meaningful way, then I must climb the tree and reach for it. I also realized that I must risk much, while avoiding the numerous personal traps and pitfalls that I encounter, in order to invest myself wholly in the process. The scariest part for me was wanting this educational change to happen enough to "LET GO"! Little did I know, during that retreat, that I was being prepared, rested, and strengthened for an intensely challenging journey ahead. A journey that at every turn would bring a new tree, a luscious banana, and another opportunity to let go!

"Some of us think holding on makes us strong; but sometimes it is letting go." Hermann Hesse

Perspective: Swaz

"Two heads are better than one." Although a well-known cliché, this phrase could not be more à propos in the organization of our new course. In February 2008, Mary Ellen presented to me the concept of her "Media Literacy Class" and offered that we team teach it. I was intrigued. I told her that I would think about it, reflect upon it, make a list of pros and cons and evaluate what I could contribute to this new venture. Five minutes later, I was on board! Such is the power of a great idea, an idea that rings true immediately, an idea that has so much potential that it draws you in at once.

World Class

As it turned out, and for scheduling reasons, I was going to be one of three teachers involved. Mary Ellen would be the common denominator and spend two periods a day with the class. Brenda Blue, her nickname based on her loving and highly empathetic personality, and I would each cover one of the two periods allocated to the course. The final composition of the course would include three teachers with diverse backgrounds; an art teacher, a French teacher and a health teacher.

One can easily rationalize the idea of team teaching any course. There would be three of us instead of one, to do the following:

- plan lessons
- discuss the curriculum
- brainstream ways to improve the course
- assess students' projects
- divide up tasks based on each person's comfort zone and expertise
- decide on the best, most effective, team combination of students

In a nutshell, three brains would most definitely maximize output and offer diverse viewpoints. Since there would be at least two of us in the classroom at all times, we could accommodate 35-40 students in one section and provide the media literacy experience to a greater number of interested individuals. After teaching the course for two semesters, I learned that the team of teachers is effective much beyond the aforementioned list of shared responsibilities. By its sheer nature, this is a class that necessitates much organization. As students choose and develop their projects, it takes several teachers to guide them in the proper direction, to attend to their needs, to establish contacts with the outside world, etc. If one of us failed to cover one area, another would pick up the slack. This is the pure beauty of such an experience. Since we all have similar work ethics and teaching philosophies, we tend to work equally hard. We communicate when we are not able to offer our very best because of personal or professional obligations and we always make sure that the bases are covered. Our students have understood that this is not a traditional class and that we run it as we would a small business. Even the language we use has evolved to reflect the language of the business world. We are supervisors and they are our employees. What they do reflects upon us, collectively, and upon our "company." There is a level of professionalism that must be attained and maintained by all. In setting the bar as high as we can, we have been able to motivate students to produce the very best of products and to present them in the most skilled way. We also have been able to aim for a level of respect and understanding rarely observed in typical classroom settings. None of that could ever have happened with one of us running the show. As we were designing the course, it became evident that we needed a double period to meet our needs. This would be a course subdivided into the following integral segments: introduction of material; tech mini-lessons; media viewing and analysis; and project planning, designing, producing, and presenting. The traditional 40 minute class period would certainly not allow us adequate time to effectively cover that which was necessary to accomplish our short term goals. Students would be expected to network with other teams, to assign roles, to divide up tasks, to write a detailed proposal, to create products, and to present their work to the class, the school, and/or the community. All of that takes time, much more than 40 minutes. There would also need to be built-in time to get the computers up and running and to clean up at the end of each session.

The program was eventually designed to include the designation of two class periods, back to back, at the start of the day. For one semester, this would allow for an enrollment of 40 interested students. If successful, the second semester would allow for the enrollment of 40 more eager students.

CHAPTER 7

The earth is frozen solid.

The 4 "P's"
The backbone of the cours

"Knowledge is experience, everything else is information."   Albert Einstein

Perspective: Swaz

As Don Tapscott explains in "Grown Up Digital," (Tapscott, Don (2008) How the Net Generation is Changing Your World. McGraw Hill Co., New York) there are 8 Net Generation Norms. They are as follows:

1. **freedom/** liberty
2. **customization/** personalization
3. **scrutiny/** transparency
4. **integrity/** openness
5. **entertainment/** play
6. **collaboration/** relationship
7. **speed/** instant gratification
8. **innovation/** originality

On day one, we introduced the eight norms by sharing the following statements with our new group of students.

This is how our course embraces these norms:

1. You will be **free** to choose your own topics and products.

2. You will be able to **customize** everything to meet your needs and style.

3. You will have a chance to **critique** the work of others.

4. You will be **accountable** to your teammates and supervisors.

5. You will have **fun** creating original products that reflect your viewpoints.

6. You will always work **within a team.**

7. You will have the chance to work at your **own pace.**

8. You will come up with **new ideas** to make our world a better place.

The new, positive view that we invited the students to embrace could be summarized with the following acrostic:

Openness

Play

Transparency

Immunity (freedom)

Modification (customize)

Innovation

Speed

Team

Perspective: Mary Ellen

What is it that could be so drastically different in a 21st century classroom versus the classrooms of the last century? As we have already identified, the need to shift from an Industrial Age model to an Information Age model is key. I once had a professor who would constantly ask her students, "What would that look like?" This question and the importance of its implication have been settling into my bones ever since. So, what would 21st century learning look like? How would we design the day to day events that would culminate into the learning experience that would prepare our students to be global citizens? Let me begin with shifting and redefining the roles of the stake holders and then detail the basic elements that make up the classroom.

Teacher: The teacher's role shifts from one who disseminates information and tests to one who supervises the gathering of information. The teacher guides the educational process through the phases of *brainstreaming*, team collaboration, proposals, production, presentation, and reflection.

Collaborative teaching is utilized for two purposes: to model desired interactions from students in the classroom and to mirror the responsibilities of team work in a global society.

Students: The student's role shifts from an independent agent to an intricate and valued part of a whole team. The student works and contributes as a team member but is assessed as an individual contributor. The shift of student assessment, therefore, moves from a focus on the student's weak areas (needing to be strengthened) to looking for the student's strengths that can be built upon. The student is encouraged to shift self-analysis from how they can manage their weaknesses to how they can maximize the use of their strengths to benefit the team. The student is accepted and celebrated for who s/he is upon arrival to class. Through supervisors' modeling, the teams genuinely share knowledge, talents, and expertise. This process allows students to gradually and naturally learn from one another. It allows for improving areas of weakness while assimilating new skills at a personal pace.

Teams: Students are observed and pre-assessed to determine initial academic, social, and technical strengths. Teams are designated by the supervisors so that each group is comprised of students of diverse strengths. Areas that are identified most often include leadership and facilitation skills, creative and technical skills, task-oriented or organizational skills, and public speaking or presentation skills. Students work collaboratively to plan but may often work independently within the boundaries set by the team. Students are taught a teaming process and are engaged in self and team assessments at regular intervals throughout their work together.

Now that you have a good idea of what the new roles of teachers, students, and teams would look like in the 21st century classroom, you may wonder how the content will be packaged.

World Class

Content: Classes can be based on non-specific content areas. With various exploratory possibilities under the umbrella of broader subjects (such as our Media Literacy Class), the content can be skill-based or theme-based. Content specific classes may choose to maintain the core topics and themes of the traditional 20th century model, but may choose to integrate team and personal choices for research or presentation. Supervisors may wish to pre-organize choices so that teams represent all content areas in need of mastery.

Skills: Once we accept that the only constant in our world is change, then it becomes easier to let go of the idea that we must master task-oriented or information specific skills. Rather, it becomes easier for us to digest the notion that the skills worth mastering are primarily the less tangible and harder to measure. Skills of information gathering, problem-solving, inter and intra-personal communication skills, associative thinking, self-reflection, and observational capabilities are all important beyond compare. Emotional intelligence, specifically the increased ability to empathize, is more essential to our survival than ever before. Global citizenship evolved due to the dramatic increase in communication made possible by technology. With our new global citizenship comes the shared responsibility to be productive, contributing members of a society that we promote to be safe, healthy, and fulfilling for all.

Our new course was to be titled "I am a Citizen of the World" (a course of study in media literacy and social issues). We felt that it was important for the students' scope of understanding to stretch beyond their personal experience. Yet, we reasoned that, in order to understand the world, we must begin with understanding ourselves within the context of our immediate surroundings. Justifiably, we began our course with a local unit of study. We then wished to nurture our students' empathetic sensitivities by having them explore national issues. The third phase of our course was to bring students beyond ethnocentric views to global connectedness and understanding.

The 21st century is all about process and the process is all about networking. Imagine the shifts that have already occurred in education through the lens of a 90-year-old American. For the sake of this exercise, let's call her Myrtle Rose. Myrtle may have first attended a one-room schoolhouse with a class of 20 other students with ages ranging from six to fourteen years old. Reading and writing were the essentials and proper manners, arithmetic, and hygiene were other curricular highlights. Lunches were shared among the families and all children scurried home to help with the afternoon chores. The idea of sports was the stickball game at recess!

By the time Myrtle was ten, her family had moved from rural country to a city so that Dad could find work during the Depression. While Mom was home washing laundry and hanging it out on the line to dry, Myrtle attended her first public school. Myrtle would sit quietly at her desk, hands folded as instructed. She would recite memorized facts in line with various subjects she was studying. Myrtle's parents would buy her the mandated school uniform, secondhand, and then pass it along to Myrtle's younger sister. Her older brother Harry had to drop out of school to find work and to contribute to that which would be meager pickings at the dinner table. Play time was now out in the streets of the immigrant segregated neighborhoods, where the art of dodging people, objects, and a few cars, during stickball, was revered. Walking to the grocery store or church and sitting as a family around the dinner table brought a calm rhythmic routine to Myrtle's new surroundings. When Myrtle became of age, she worked in the factories while all the men were off battling a war. Her younger siblings now practiced bomb drills at school by getting under their desks.

Myrtle grew up and now her children practiced riot drills between science, Latin, math and English classes. The Civil Rights movement brought an end to segregation and the beginning of a painful era towards healing. Art was not usually offered, although physical education classes and organized school sports grew swiftly in popularity. Business classes and typing skills were second to home economics. All young women were expected to take these courses. Young men, on the other hand, took auto mechanics and woodworking.

World Class

A decade later, along with the controversy of the Vietnam War tearing the country apart, Myrtle fought for her parental control. Many obstacles were in her way. As she visited her children at college, she saw them wearing torn and faded blue jeans as well as leather headbands. Myrtle saw pot smoking and what was referred to as free love. That was mild, compared to Myrtle witnessing a whole group of students gathering on the quad to protest the war. She also witnessed the first generation to collectively rebel against authority and realized that life as she knew it would never be the same.

With the nest empty, Myrtle went to work to earn some of the finer things in life. Years passed and Myrtle now attended her grandchildren's concerts and various sporting events. She was in silent awe of the manicured lawns of the schools, the night lights, and the uniformed players on the fields. It wasn't until she attended open house and saw the difference, with her own two eyes, that she began to understand the changes that had occurred in our schools and society. Science labs, calculators, and even sex education all illuminated the changes. The classrooms' desks were now in semi-circles instead of rows. Thank goodness that Myrtle could still find comfort in the essays and posters that hung on the walls to proudly display her grandchildren's work. The last time Myrtle saw what was going on in schools was when her great grandchildren shared pictures from cell phones and pulled up a few class websites. Myrtle's eyes grew very large in her now sunken and bony face. Her eyes softened with familiarity when Myrtle saw pictures of students sitting at their desks and looking towards the front of the classroom. The students were seated in similar fashion to how she recalled being seated years ago. "Thank goodness," she sighed, "that some things don't change!"

Although it would have shocked Myrtle, the 21st century classroom pictures could have revealed all of the students working in clusters, in a state of constant dialogue and exchange of ideas. In the business world this is known as networking. Perhaps at some point in the future, we will not even house students within the confines of school buildings. In a society where both parents usually work and families live hundreds of miles apart from one another, 21st century students might gather with supervisors in and around various community arenas. This would allow them to engage in an educational process that is fully geared towards improving the lives of one another, including our global brothers and sisters. Perhaps one such gathering place would be an assisted-living complex. I think Myrtle would appreciate and find comfort in that.

THE FOUR P'S

P is for Process

It's all about process! The following is a simplification of the 21st century classroom process. Even under current mandates, we have been able to develop and initiate what we believe is a flexible educational equation to meet the needs of diverse disciplines and diverse learners.

<u>21st century World Class learning equation:</u>

(inspiration + collaboration + teaming)

+

(proposal + research + creation)

+

(presentation + assessment + reflection)

= Knowledge

Inspiration

Inspiration is to lead students into the topic or theme through storytelling, multimedia examples and other invitational approaches. The teachers' intention of empowering students to create new and personal discoveries, as they embark on their educational journey, marks the difference between inspiration and anticipatory sets. Inspiration also implies empowering the students to go beyond information gathering to the utilization of their research and products as a means to create change through action.

Collaboration: *Two heads are better than one.*

Collaboration emphasizes the value of asking for opinions and demonstrates the power of groups in generating creative solutions to problems. It encourages the development and greater use of the right side of the brain's intuitive powers to invent imaginative solutions while engaging the left side of the brain's analytical powers. Collaborative work implies that we, as educators, will accept our personal limitations and embrace our diverse strengths. It models that which should be acknowledged and celebrated in our students. This acknowledgement encourages students to release fears of inadequacy and to embrace their personal strengths as a valued way to contribute. Collaboration is how we learn to work smarter not harder.

Teaming Process: © Sheive and Metivier

Effective teaming must be taught and is essential to the success of the student. The teaming process developed by Sheive and Metivier gives a clear, five-step method, which has been used for teacher and administrative training at the State University of New York at Oswego, Educational Administration Programs.

5 Steps of Teaming

Adapted from Sheive and Metivier © 1994

<u>Roles</u>:

- <u>Facilitator</u> - leads team discussions by keeping all members on topic while soliciting input from all, using roundtable style
- <u>Timekeeper</u> - monitors time limits
- <u>Recorder</u> - documents all discussions
- <u>Reporter</u> - conveys decisions to the team, audience and/or supervisor.

Step 1: **Brainstreaming** (When everyone shares initial ideas)

The facilitator asks each team member for their idea. The timekeeper limits each person's response time. The facilitator may go *roundtable* more than once until each member has shared all of his/ her ideas.

Step 2: **Clarifying**

Clarifying is the opportunity for each team member to share what s/he meant by what s/he said while brain*streaming*. This ensures thorough communication.

The facilitator asks, "Does anyone need clarification on anything discussed in our brain*streaming* session?"

The timekeeper limits each person's response time.

The facilitator may go *roundtable* more than once until each team member is satisfied.

Step 3: **Clustering**

Clustering is putting brain*streamed* ideas into categories. It makes the database more manageable and generates new insights.

Clustering may be done by a whole team or by a few team members, as long as the results are reported and agreed upon by the entire team.

The facilitator asks the team to create categories from topics that have surfaced in the brain*streaming* session.

Step 4: **Prioritizing**

Prioritizing is looking at categories and picking those that are most meaningful, measurable, and attainable.

Step 5: **Creating graphs & charts**

This process allows for decision making regarding what kinds of graphs or charts the team wants to use to organize their ideas. They could opt to use mind maps (for example, Inspiration software or websites such as bubbl.us or mindomo), time lines, calendars, bars and column grids, excel charts, Wordles, etc*.

* As we write these lines, we are fully aware that by the time you read this, there will likely be many new tools to help organize ideas.

P is for Proposal

Propose/ Research/ Create: These processes allow one to honor each individual's strengths while practicing the teaming process. The students are guided to engage in dialogue to develop team ideas and plans. This results in a written document that is proposed to the supervisors. The only mandate is that the proposal clearly fit within one of the three appropriate units of study; local, national, or global. Within their groups, students craft a "driving question" that will give direction to their entire project and product. The driving question is typically open-ended and combines topic information and positive intent. Proposals become a living document that outlines the group's topics, job descriptions, timelines, and intended outcomes. Students divide the workload to contribute towards the final product and presentation. Once the proposal has been approved by the supervisors, the team embarks on their research and the creative process begins.

PROPOSAL CHECKLIST   TEAM#_____

I IDEAS

1. Title page (project name/ team members)
2. Goal/ driving question/ positive impact
3. Type of product
4. TITA (Identify Topic/ Intent/ Text/ Audience)
5. Team members' strengths
6. Team members' general jobs
7. Technology to be used
8. Team resources (locations/non-tech equipment/ people to interview, etc.)

II WORK

1. Title page (project name/ team members' names)
2. Job titles and detailed descriptions
3. Permission slips (for leaving room, etc.)
4. Details about presentation (script, lighting, entrance, etc.)

World Class

P is for Product

Wordreference.com defines the word product as *"an artifact that has been created by someone or some process."* In our book, a product is a support for the message that the group wants to convey and fits within a very wide range of categories. A product can be, but is not limited to, the following:

- a video
- a commercial
- a song
- a play
- a poem
- an article
- a T-shirt
- a poster
- a painting
- a collage
- an assembly
- a fundraiser (or other action based products)
- any combination from the above list.

Regardless of what product a team decides to create, there has to be a technological component. If the artifact is not digital, per se, then digital documentation must be included. Students can film their play, take photos of their paintings, prepare an iron-on design for their T-shirts, or record and manipulate their song, digitally. Following the submission of their pre-approved proposal, students begin to work. The leader/facilitator organizes the crew. The researchers start to explore online resources. The tech expert delves into the software that will be used to produce the artifact, and the creator develops some ideas regarding how to make the product original, unique, and meaningful. Looking ahead, the presentation director starts writing a script and developing some ideas on how the product would come to life for the audience on presentation day. For about eight days, the groups are hard at work meeting their deadlines. The supervisors make their rounds, inquire about progress, answer questions, encourage individual students, guide and mediate, help troubleshoot, give suggestions, steer in one direction or another, cheer on and/or dissuade. The artifacts then come to life. They are powerful, political, and poignant. They are human, humorous, and happy. They are aesthetic, emotional, and incredible. They are raw but full of promise. Day after day, they become more chiseled. One day, usually just before the deadline, they are ready. Examples of products included are as follows: an article addressing the inequity of disciplinary procedures at our school for our local strand; a film about the power of the media for our national strand; a video about the genocide in Darfur, a rap addressing global warming, and a series of speeches molded into a film regarding gay rights around the world, for our international strand. They are beautiful and sad, but they are all original, and are all based on the opportunity offered by this class. Through the teaming of individuals, ideas arise and a project is born. A product is completed for all to benefit from on presentation day.

P is for Presentation

The supervisors create a schedule. On the first day of presentations, groups one, two, and three present. On the second day groups four, five, and six, etc. We require students to use the days leading up to presentation time to "practice." "P" is also for Practice, an element of the process that proves essential but is unfortunately underestimated by the groups until glitches start to occur on THE day. Practice consists of the following: testing the equipment, including the computer(s) and the files/ links that will be used; testing the microphones, and any other tools that are needed; practicing the script at the microphone; doing a full run-through as one would at a dress rehearsal before a show; and making sure that each job has been filled and that each person is fully aware of and confident in his/her role.

Typically, presentations include the following: an introduction or preface by some or all group members; a showing of the product(s); and a conclusion. Students and supervisors rate presentations with the help of a rubric. At the end of each presentation, the whole class does a full critique. The group members face the audience to accept the evaluation made by the entire class.

Although the three essential components of our projects are deemed essential, we find that our schools typically come up short when it comes to presentation and reflection. Including presentation, assessment, and reflection helps to bring about and reinforce accountability and continued dialogue. This results in reflective practices and growth. Rubrics for presentations and critiques are utilized to guide students toward higher quality experiences. Providing an audience (especially outside of the traditional classroom) proves to be a *most* powerful tool with regard to assuring the highest level of meaningful engagement.

Presentation example

Topic: Gay rights around the world

Category: Social justice, global unit

Starring: Students A, B, C & D

Written by: Student A

Directed by: Student C

     Gay people are still persecuted in many countries. This group looks at specific examples of homosexual men and women around the world whose sexual orientation leads to victimization, a sex change, or death. The movie features individuals from Turkey, Uganda, the Netherlands, and the United States. As the students examine these real cases, they also offer a message of hope for everyone to be free to love their partners in an open world.

PRESENTATION RUBRIC FOR SUPERVISORS

1. TECH/ STAGING PRIOR TO PRESENTATION

Both tested on _____/ One tested on _____/ None tested _____

2. INTRO. / PREFACE TO PRESENTATION

Indicates background, purpose, and intended outcome _ / Indicates 2 of the 3 _/ Indicates 1 or none of the 3_

QUALITY OF PRODUCT:

3. VISUAL QUALITY

Clear and appealing to the eye ___/ Not so clear and/ or not appealing to the eye ___/ Poor visual quality ___

4. AUDIO QUALITY

Clear and appealing to the ear ___/ Not so clear and/ or not appealing to the ear ___/ Poor audio quality ___

INTEGRITY OF THE MESSAGE:

5. Is it school audience appropriate?

yes   questionable   no

6. Does it address the issues at the proper level (local/ national/ international)? yes   in part   no

7. Is the intent clearly presented?

yes   in part   no

8. Are solutions and possibilities clearly offered?

yes   somewhat   no

9. SOURCES & COPYRIGHT

Clearly documented   Somewhat documented   Missing

10. USE OF TECHNOLOGY

Very meaningful   Somewhat meaningful

Technology does not support the intent of the project

11. CONCLUSION

Strong conclusion clearly wraps up the presentation

Conclusion has limited impact   Weak conclusion

BONUS: TRANSCENDS FROM PRESENTATION TO ACTION

World Class

P is also for Perspective Piron (Swaz):

"P" is also for presentations to the public. Presentations are designed to show the community what the students have produced, to connect with the world beyond students and teachers, and to give our class a true voice, one that extends further than the walls of the classroom. As one of our community presentations ends, I reflect upon the process we have undertaken. Imagine an auditorium. House lights off. On stage, a couch and an armchair. The supervisors are quietly watching the show, a culmination of student efforts for the semester, including products on stereotyping, civil rights, global warming, and gay rights. They are taking in the months of work and looking at the big picture that their students created. The conclusion of this amazing presentation, a black and white movie, is playing on the screen. A song, "Let it be," plays as the audio background for the film. One of the students is singing the famous Beatles song and his voice is soft and smooth. As the movie plays, students leave their seats and start going up on stage, one by one. They stand facing the film, their backs to the audience. They stand tall and proud, dignified. Their dark silhouettes, solemn. The moment rings so true and so meaningful that the supervisors are moved beyond belief. "This is really what it's all about," they think, with smiles on their faces and tears in their eyes.

CHAPTER 8

The snow geese arrived, first just a few, before long the flock.

Teaming

"Be yourself, everyone else is taken."

Oscar Wilde

I could see the raft of Canadian geese floating near shore, insulated from the icy waters of Lake Ontario. What was that in the middle of the dark formation? It was a swan, oblivious to the difference between itself and the geese that surrounded it. As it comfortably floated, it was happy to be protected.

Perspective: Mary Ellen

Teaming is not as easy as one may think. Even with our handy-dandy teaming process, gifted to us by professors Sheive and Metivier ©, teaming can be a rugged and painful process. The experience of the teaming journey really depends upon our acceptance of individual differences. A popular slogan in education during the past fifteen years has been, "Teach Tolerance." I say that there is a better approach. "Teach tolerance" implies that one is better than another and therefore one should *tolerate* one another. The following stories illustrate the differences between tolerance and acceptance. This realization helped to formulate how and why we emphasize teaming as an essential component of the 21st century classroom and beyond!

Diversity

In chapter two we discussed our "Diversity Project." It became the driving force that led us to develop our new course. What we didn't share with you, though, was that when our diversity project was presented to a larger assembly style audience, the reception was not completely positive. One presentation, expressing acceptance of people's various styles and sexual orientations, was met with resistance. This resulted in a personal threat being directed towards the creator of the piece. It was our first lesson as supervisors regarding the awesome responsibility we must bear when promoting diversity and acceptance of individual differences. Our Civil Rights leaders know, all too well, the hostility that seeps out of the recesses of people's ignorant minds. People with insecurity often attempt to undermine that which they perceive to be a threat. Our second lesson came as another student, inspired by the diversity project, came to speak to me one day.

Journal entry: Mary Ellen - May 21, 2008

Margaret sashays into my room, her long, free-form curls trailing behind her. She pauses at the first large table in my classroom and plops her stuff down exclaiming, "Shevalier, I can't believe you weren't here last week. I really needed to share this with you. I couldn't believe you weren't here." My eyes, peering up from my computer, fixed on hers. I could see the energy that her built up facial gestures contained. The muscles in her face turned up one corner of her mouth into an amused half smile. I asked, "What is it, Margaret? What's happened?" She replied, "I went on this peace walk and I knew you would love it. I met all these people and I told them about your course and ..." Her story went on in a long, run-on sentence, and she continued with wide-eyed enthusiasm, "It was great!" She took a deep breath to replace the oxygen she had depleted. My heart was beginning to speed up as a reaction to her undeniably raw and pure passion for a cause she was convinced was honorable. Is this why my blood pressure rose? She then fished out, from her embroidered, striped, and flowered orange, blue, and brown fabric purse, a book entitled <u>Warrior Writers</u>. My eyes moistened with tears. All in one moment, the joy, fear, anticipation, and responsibility of my choices bore down heavily upon me in an overwhelming flood of emotion that caused me to stutter. In my attempt to process this surge, I staggered, reaching my hands in front of me to indicate to Margaret to please pause for a moment as I regrouped. I reached for a Kleenex saying, "I'm going to cry." Unashamed of my transparency, I openly put a voice to the rambling mixture of thoughts and emotion stirring inside of me like a smoothie of crushed ice, yogurt, fresh parsley, and lemon juice. I started, "I am feeling more like your parent. I am afraid for you, for what I know and what you don't know. I honor and respect your intentions but be careful. I'm crying too, because just yesterday, Piron called me and said that we have to write a book. I told her, 'I am.' Then you showed me this, <u>Warrior Writers</u>. I feel the convergence." While crying and talking at the same time, I said, "It seems that people are ready for change and healing." Margaret, undaunted and maybe even pleased by her presentation's effect on me, went on to tell me of the people she met as she participated in the peace walk from Adams, NY to Watertown, NY (roughly 15 miles).

Our closure included some motherly advice. Interrupting me, Margaret emphasized her delight at belonging to a cause, an honorable cause. "Margaret", I insisted, "don't forget to question everything. Be an independent thinker. As honorable as your intent is, is this how you want to be involved? Is it the best for you? Who are these people? What are their motives? Are you willing to be guilty by association in the event that something goes awry? What are their personal habits? Is there any danger of drinking and/or drug usage? Make a list of your core beliefs about peace, a list of your boundaries, and the pros and cons of this particular way of expressing it. Be an independent thinker. Be careful. Be safe!"

My heart opened further this day. My mind, while trying to stay in denial, just couldn't. It whispered softly, "You reap what you sow, tend the garden carefully and be cautious with these young, impressionable minds."

How could our work to promote unity end up as a threat to the safety of one of our students? I pondered this notion, often losing sleep. I found myself looking at the faces that passed by me in the halls differently, as if I could find the answer by reading them. Then it struck me. One cannot accept our differences without the ability to first empathize! We did it wrong. We need to promote empathy before we will ever stand a chance of convincing our youth to promote acceptance within their world. Without wasting time, I presented my idea to our school's steering committee. I had been invited to attend the meeting with the intention that I would get involved in facilitating a building-wide promotion of character education. I gladly obliged with the condition that empathy be the focus of this initiative. "Step into my Shoes" became our slogan and the students reentered a new school year greeted by a display in the main foyer. This display was comprised of shoe boxes and rows of dress shoes, men's shoes, women's shoes, flip-flops, dress boots, work boots, sneakers, oxfords, loafers, pumps, and more! That was our kick off (excuse the pun). For the remainder of the year, we posted various reminders and promoted many activities to increase our empathy and to sensitize our students regarding our treatment and judgment of others. The harvest from the year's efforts seemed to be changed perceptions or, at least, increased sensitivity. Later in the year, students artistically created media projects to address empathy issues such as weight, race, religion, sexual orientation, economic status, etc.

Teaching tolerance, therefore, was beneath our goal. We realized that once the seeds of empathy were planted and nurtured, it was possible for us to surpass the notion of simply tolerating our differences. With the groundwork laid, we could embrace and celebrate differences. Again, my ideas for the new course were reinforced. In order to become a citizen of the world, we must celebrate the value of our cultural differences and nurture an outward appreciation of one another. In so doing, we are healing the world, beginning with the healing of our own hearts.

What did embracing our differences through the teaming process look like in our classroom? We knew it would be a challenge but we were ready to break down the walls.

Journal entry: Mary Ellen - Nov. 2009

I turned around quickly to double-check whether or not our mobile computers had been returned to our lock and key cabinet. To my surprise, there was John, all six feet of him, flipping me the bird with vigor. "Did you just flip me off?" I asked, in a bit of a shock. "Yes," he replied. (Just as shocked that I had caught him.) "Thanks for your honesty," I blurted out with a nervous, loud laugh. John turned and took three steps toward his seat. I called out, "Hold it, John." I waited for him to face me. "Why did you flip me off?" I asked. John paused and tried to find the words to explain. His frustration tolerance was obviously exceeded. As he mingled his anger with his explanation, he stated, "My team thinks I'm a big slacker and no matter what I do, it's not enough and they don't believe I am doing my work." I watched pain wash over his face and down his arms until his large hands were clenched. I took a deep breath and replied, "I'm sorry, but why are you flipping me off?" John was deflated and was relieved to see a human being temporarily standing in front of him. His frustration stemmed from being unable to articulate that I was the one responsible for his failing team dynamic. By design, the process takes responsibility out of the teachers' hands and places accountability into the hands of the students. This just *really ticked him off.*

Virtual Board Meetings

After each unit of study we paused for a board meeting in which every student could voice his/her opinions regarding what was or was not working in the class. We used various strategies to help students to prepare their thoughts and to give them a chance to express their views in a non-threatening format. At first, it appeared as if students were saying what they thought we wanted to hear. Later, their honesty, depth, and breadth of opinion increased to our pleasure (and education)! We addressed each concern, within a day, bullet by bullet. We did so in an honest and open fashion. Students appeared to appreciate our candid consideration of their views. We believe it empowered them to accept a higher level of ownership. We *know* that it helped us to improve the course and our approach with each group.

Here are some examples of the feedback we received from our students. We separated our discussions under the topics of process, teams, and products/presentations.

Process

- More cooperation between team members needed
- More communication and guidance from supervisors needed
- Too much teaching from supervisors; not enough time for production
- More clarity and direction of expectations
- Less documentation should be needed
- Unit one too overwhelming
- Everyone in group needs to help and physically stay with group
- Need more practice time
- Better division of responsibilities decided by team
- Make sure product is truly finished by due date
- Team meetings at beginning of class to decide what needs to be done that day
- Try an assembly line format to complete a product
- One thumbdrive with everything on it

Teams

- Bigger teams
- Everyone in group needs to meet own responsibility and physically stay with group

- Much more and much better communication needed between team members
- Team meetings at beginning and end of class to start class off with goals and end with reflection
- Age differences make it difficult
- More or harsher consequences for individuals not upholding their responsibilities

Products and Presentations
- Provide a list of ideas for products
- Provide tutorials to help with using technology
- Teach us cool technology stuff
- More practice time needed to get ready for presentations
- Only have us do one product
- Present to a larger and older audience
- More original products, think outside-the-box
- Products need to make a point and take action, not just a show-and-tell
- Provide time for other groups to critique products prior to due date and make suggestions
- Better effects in the products
- Better lighting and sound for presentations

Slacker Be Gone

It became apparent that students would either respect the teaming process and maneuver successfully or they would openly or passively resist teaming and be a blocker or slacker to the detriment of their team.

A new procedure was conceived through brain*streaming* to give teams professional tools to deal with negative and/or counter-productive behavior. The Slacker Be Gone form was unveiled the day after one of our student *Board Meetings* as a result of numerous complaints from team members. To our relief, the majority of our 34 students clapped and laughed at the unveiling of the Slacker Be Gone policy/ form. A few students shamefully sank lower into their seats. The three step procedure empowered the students. It ushered them into adult decision making and personal choices, yet it gave them the safety net of their supervisors' being the disciplinarians when necessary.

Slacker Be Gone!

Re-designed team strategies, Nov. 1, 2008

The following strategies have been reviewed by and agreed upon by our team.

1. If someone does not meet their agreed upon responsibility, the team will bring it up and provide documentation. Upon completing said documentation, the whole team will allow for identified slackers to make up work. The expected due date will be specified in the meeting minutes (*consider documenting details of the quality of the job expected if you fear that may be an issue*).

2. If the work is not done by the specified deadline, the team confronts the slacker in front of the supervisor(s). This act initiates steps towards expulsion from the team.

3. The rights of the slacker will include an interview and an opportunity to defend his/her work performance with evidence.

4. The right of the team is to receive an answer within three days of reporting to the supervisor(s).

5. Reports must include justifications of the action taken.

In a scenario where students choose not to use the Slacker Be Gone protocol, the supervisors' response may be as follows. This helps to reinforce the proper use of established procedures.

Student A: Student B has done nothing at all in the group the last few days.

Supervisor: Have you started the steps on the Slacker Be Gone form?

Student A: No.

Supervisor: End of conversation.

Students must learn that the whole group is responsible for the work produced. Some control fanatics need to let the banana go and appreciate the art of delegation. Some slackers must accept that they have responsibilities and that they need to follow through accordingly. If they do not, then the group has the right to move on with the dismissal of the idler. The only stipulations are that the slacker must be given a chance to make up the work, that true communication between the group members must take place, and that proper documentation must be filed in the group's portfolio. The process provides for another great lesson in accountability.

Perspective: Swaz Spyware

As students work in teams, divide up the work, research, organize, plan, and create, they still remain teenagers. No matter how much effort we devote to teaching students about accountability and integrity, such an open forum as our class will by nature lead to some distractions. As we have seen, these students, being Net Geners, demand freedom, entertainment, collaboration, and speed while utilizing technology. In their *other world*, they want to connect with their friends and take care of some of their personal business. In our class, it was no surprise to find one student emailing a friend from a college account. Another student ordered a Barbie for a niece. A third student researched local news that was unrelated to the group's project, etc. We identified a strategy to limit such diversions. A software program called

<u>Vision</u> allows one to keep an eye on computer usage. <u>Vision</u> takes action as deemed necessary by "giving the eye" to the culprit. The program allows for the stopping of a student, in his/her tracks, from a remote location. A large eye, the logo of the software, fills in the computer screen. The computer becomes frozen and the student knows that s/he has been caught and we must have a discussion regarding the matter. Depending on the site(s) visited, the offender could be restricted from computer usage for a day, a week, or beyond. Such is the nature of the beast.

As stated previously, Net Geners typically like to scrutinize. They expect transparency and look for integrity and openness. As we developed our course, we tweaked it and improved its quality. The course began to build a positive reputation. We dared hope that students would see the benefits of remaining true to their work and teams. In honoring the commitment that they made to the class and to themselves, they were regarded with a new level of respect by their supervisors and by their peers. This elevated the quality of the work environment to a new height and allowed for better opportunities to produce valued work. The end benefit was that students learned to adopt healthy work ethics and they became more respected citizens of the world at large.

Perspective: Swaz
Microcosm for a future work ethic

Employers have made it very clear that being able to work in teams, getting along with other employees, and successfully networking for the good of the company are major strengths to be expected from new hires. We readily recognize that this is also true at our level, in a class where we have created a mini-corporation. Students must learn to work with others, learn to pool their strengths, and learn to create as a group.

We like to start one of our classes with the following bell-ringer: "What would differ if this were a job you were reporting to instead of a class?" It is interesting to listen to students share their ideas. Some focus on the lack of pressure in a school while others emphasize that in a job situation they would enjoy the work more because they would have chosen the career. A few days later, we follow up with the question, "At your job, would you expect to choose your colleagues?" Many perspectives are shared. Most think that they would have little control over who they would work with, while others believe that they would be able to select employees with whom they would work when completing special projects. These questions and discussions, regarding strengths and weaknesses and how they would come together to benefit society, would lead to the establishment of teams for our class. With the use of questionnaires (see the following example) and personality surveys as well as the daily observation of our students' interactions, we would combine our workers so as to make diverse teams that would allow for all levels of engagement to be represented.

PERSONALITY QUESTIONNAIRE

(our design, modify it according to your needs)

Rate yourself by choosing the number that best describes your personality.

Circle 1 or 2 if you match the word(s) on the left more closely, 4 or 5 if you are closer to the word(s) on the right, and choose 3 if you feel as if you belong in the middle.

creative   1 2 3 4 5 ordinary

loves tech stuff   1 2 3 4 5 tech challenged

leader   1 2 3 4 5 follower

intellectual   1 2 3 4 5 practical

conventional 1 2 3 4 5 innovative

relaxed   1 2 3 4 5 high-strung

hands-on   1 2 3 4 5 academic

thinker 1 2 3 4 5 concrete

proud   1 2 3 4 5 modest

athlete   1 2 3 4 5 reader

original   1 2 3 4 5 common

computer challenged 1 2 3 4 5 computer savvy

loner 1 2 3 4 5 social

traditional 1 2 3 4 5 eccentric

expert 1 2 3 4 5 inexperienced

independent 1 2 3 4 5 connected

ideas 1 2 3 4 5 actions

textbook learning 1 2 3 4 5 online learner

The POST IT Procedure for Picking Partners

- Acquire an array of colored post it notes.

- Find a vast flat surface to place the notes, such as a wide desk or table.

- Choose a color per role (green for facilitator, pink for tech person, etc).

- Start creating little rainbows, by positioning the colored pieces in groups with each color represented.

- Discuss combinations with your co-supervisor and assign students to roles.

- Reorganize to better match student personalities and styles.

- Admire work and hope for the best once students actually start working with their established teams!

World Class

We have found that groups of three, four, or five team members work best. There must be enough members on a team to divide up the work fairly and intelligently, but if there are too many students making up one team, then someone is bound to fall through the cracks and become a slacker.

At the end of each unit, team assessment takes place in a variety of ways. Some assessment tools include:

- ❖ Online forms whereby students rate themselves and their team members (http://www.spartanpride.org/webpages/citizen/forms.cfm);
- ❖ Compilation of various scores that translate into a grade for each individual, using rubrics that reflect how well each student works on behalf of his/her group;
- ❖ Chicken stories (see examples below);
- ❖ Team "truth essay" that allows students to reflect upon the process and honestly paint a picture of each team member's contribution.

FINAL TEAM ASSESSMENT:
THE TRUTH ESSAY

"You can model behavior but you cannot control the actions of others."

Write an essay that includes the following:

- Page 1: Unit title, team members' names, the author's name and date submitted;

- Pages 2-4: Each separate page should have each team member's name and the various roles s/he played for each process. Each team member is to detail his/her perceptions of his/her team members' contributions as weak, mediocre, or strong. They must detail evidence to support their perceptions. Each member must include a page about him/herself;

- Page 5: Each member must write a concluding paragraph that summarizes his/her overall experience as a part of the team and what s/he would like to do differently to improve his/her contributions during the next team experience.

Chicken stories

This activity is a fun way for group members to share input about the work ethics of one of their fellow team members. We give them examples such as "Why did Martin Luther King cross the road? Because he had a dream of what might be possible on the other side." "Why did Charlie Chaplin cross the road? Because he had to find his voice."

Students are asked to answer the question **"Why or how did your chicken cross the road?"**

Here are some student examples:

"My chicken was very scared to cross the road, but we encouraged him a lot and finally he made it there."

"My chicken ran across the road to catch up with her boyfriend."

"When my chicken was on the side of the road, he took out his iPhone to check for restaurants in the area."

"Why did Mary and Brian cross the road? They didn't, because they were never here."

"I escorted my chicken across the road for shopping online during class."

Journal entry: Mary Ellen - November, 2008
I have a voice and it honors who I am.

Upon review of our unit one projects, we were concerned that the majority of the teams had chosen issues revolving around the local topic of stereotyping. Not wanting to dissuade the students from exploring the topics of their choice (as promised), the teams presented what was obviously a popular theme among teens and one which they were compelled to speak about. One team created a huge, wall-sized poster that invited passersby to write words expressing how they had been stereotyped in the past. This team videotaped the participants and later made a powerful, short, video document to share people's opinions and feelings. (http://www.spartanpride.org/webpages/citizen/index.cfm?subpage=548828). Using the live signature graffiti approach again, they then created a short film entitled, "When I grow up." This film brought forth conversations regarding gender stereotyping in the workforce. They interviewed numerous students about their aspirations, highlighting those who chose fields that were considered unusual for their gender. Another team created a short but emotional film that depicted the hurt and isolation that stereotyping can cause. One other group made a film that opened with a verbal display of typical derogatory terms used when stereotyping. Finally, one astute team looked beyond their topic and asked if their project could be to arrange an assembly for our sixth through eighth graders by utilizing all the other teams' work. They would assume responsibility for getting permission, advertising, scripting, and orchestrating the event! We were pleasantly surprised by what happened our first semester, with our first unit of study, and our first group of students. We were simply blown away, but we didn't have time to stay in that state of mind for long because there was much work to be done! On October 28, 2008, the media literacy students successfully hosted their main event. The following is an excerpt of what was on the student-designed flyer that went to all of the middle school teachers:

The Re-education of America

"We hope to educate students on the negative effects of stereotyping in our schools. This assembly will consist of short movies, posters, and oral presentations depicting the harmful effects of stereotyping. As high school students we hope to act as positive role models and guide middle school students in the right direction while teaching them how important it is to live with an open mind and a sense of civility."

As the middle school students entered the auditorium, they found themselves in a strange and intimidating atmosphere. The student presenters lined the aisles of the auditorium and whispered stereotypical slurs at the middle school students as they passed. Our audience, students, and teachers alike, was affronted by name-calling such as "jock, prep, emo, goth, punk, nerd, geek, goody-goody, loser, popular," etc. Certainly, the high school students had their guests' attention but before the latter could sit down, they were directed to walk up and around the stage to view the various posters and signs that were created. The teachers were directed to walk a different route, one that brought them to a table that donned professional presentation cases that contained student proposals, communiqués, and justifications for their work. Fully engaged by what educators would refer to as an *anticipatory set*, the audience members found a seat and attentively awaited more!

Here are excerpts from the actual script. Each bullet represents a line uttered by a student.

- MC – Welcome everyone to the very first "I am a Citizen of the World Assembly," a course of study in Media Literacy.
- What is Media?
- It's material or a way of communicating with others.
- Such as – commercials, articles, posters, t-shirts, movies, and music.
- What is Literacy?
- It means to read or interpret information.
- Why do we want to learn to read or interpret various media?

- Because it surrounds us.

- Because it influences us.

- Because it impacts us.

- Why do we want to look at media with critical eyes and ears?

- Because if we can take it in wisely, we can make our own choices.

- If we can make our own choices, we can begin to think for ourselves.

- If we can think for ourselves, we can begin to express ourselves.

- If we can express ourselves using various forms of media, we have a voice.

- And if we have a voice, we can and will be heard.

- Please enjoy OUR voices today on the issue of stereotyping. The following presentations express our views.

- Students, we want you to be ready to think for yourselves and later reflect upon what you have seen and heard today. Maybe you can write about it or have conversations about it.

- Teachers, try to read between the lines and appreciate the process while you view today's presentation. It has been one heck of a process and to stand before you today, sharing our work, makes it all worthwhile. Our voices are being heard.

(Screen scrolls names of 4 teams followed by their movies.)

After the films, the live commentary resumed.

All (MLC) students were lined up on stage. They concluded the assembly with the following parting words:

- Thank you for listening to our voices. We invite you to write to us and to send us your feedback. Please visit our blog at

www.spartanpride.org/webpages/citizen/myblog.cfm

- Remember – don't stereotype, it's ignorant!

- Stereotyping makes you not cool.

- Please celebrate your differences because

And for their final line, the entire class chimed in:

- You are all citizens of the world!

We had a few minutes to take questions and comments from the students before we concluded. Several youngsters raised their hands, eager to advance to the microphone. One sixth grade boy, rising on his tippy toes to reach the podium, said, "It was difficult to walk past the students calling us names. I felt quite insulted." Then, a beautifully confident sixth grade girl approached the podium. Her eyes turned to the high school students who lined the stage, and she told them that kids her age

167

look up to them. Since they were saying that stereotyping is un-cool, she believed them and would model after them. It was then that my eyes filled with tears of joy and astonishment as did the eyes of my colleagues. I whispered to them, "It doesn't get any better than this."

Journal Entry: Mary Ellen - January 2009

Awestruck, I reflect on how swiftly and seamlessly the first half of this year has passed. On the back burner of my mind, simmering softly is the awareness of the support that came to us from all directions to make our new course a reality. Surfacing in my daily thoughts are the many people whose faith, good intentions, and hard work have contributed to a new and exciting educational adventure for our media literacy students as well as a brighter future for the South Jefferson Central School District as a whole.

It seems like yesterday that we sat in the principal's office expressing the four year plan to implement and grow a 21st century course entitled,

"I am a Citizen of the World" (a course of study in media literacy). Our principal was attentive. Our guidance counselor was formulating. Swaz was open to the newness. Brenda, our health teacher, was ready to assist. That was in February of 2008, one year ago. Today I am right on track with my plan. The experience has surpassed my expectations and is more than I could have ever dreamed possible.

February to June brought a flurry of meetings bringing our superintendent, assistant principal, district technology leader, professors from Oswego, and others on board. We connected with CILC (Center for Interactive Learning and Collaboration) and arranged for national and international video conferences in the upcoming year. We wrote grants, one resulting in a DAALI (Digital Arts Alliance Leadership Institute) workshop in technology. The other grants were rejected and put on the shelf to be resurrected at a later time or date. Our administration found a way to provide us with a classroom, necessary equipment, and the encouragement that we needed to move forward. It was no small feat for all of those who supported us to forge the path so that we might find our way clear to our classroom of the future.

The most intense, exciting, and exhausting meetings came from brain*streaming* with my two teammates for detailed ideas to speckle the outlined formula I had designed. We joyfully questioned, pondered, and developed what was soon to become a very engaging curriculum for our first batch of students.

September came with a crisp mixture of anxiety and enthusiasm as we opened our new course in the auditorium with 35 students. The class was a beautifully eclectic mix of grade levels, GPA's, social groupings, and talents. We were not disappointed by the students' willingness to embrace the new class format and content.

The presence of two student teachers, who were conducting a graduate research project under the direction of Dr. J. Kibbey, helped us to create a unique learning community. The roles of our students, teachers, student teachers, and supervisors became melded in ways that made us all a perfect circle of life learners.

December brought forth the cold chills of winter but we were warmed by the glow of satisfaction as we listened to the student teachers' research presentation. There were many professors, educational leaders, and supporters of ingenuity in attendance. The energy was positive and electrifying. One attendee, Dr. Trainor, Assistant Superintendent for Instruction, exclaimed, (paraphrased) "I went to a conference yesterday about 21st century learning and listened to a national speaker heralding the importance of 21st century learning. Today, I'm here in Adams, NY, and you showed me exactly what it looks like."

So here we were, one year later, and the new year opened with our toughest audience, our colleagues. As I nervously, yet proudly, read my opening statement, I saw the predictable smiling faces on some of my colleagues. I also saw the downturned heads and diverted eyes of others. I could not have been more proud of my students, my teammates, and the student teachers, who so innocently stood before the mix of teachers. Many

171

of the teachers appeared apathetic, some were suspicious, and others were *secretly* supportive. During my 28 years in the field of education, I have never understood how or why teachers become so collectively resistant when attempts are made to fully and meaningfully engage students in the learning process.   Yet, teachers expect their students to be completely open to what they share with them daily, despite the lack of connectedness to their lives and their future aspirations.   Truly, I heard the pounding of my convictions beat fully alive within the deafening silence that shrouded the room on that day.

One week later, we presented again to our community.   At the conclusion of the presentation, the glow of the light-covered screen shone upon the students' young faces.   The young man who had flipped me off previously was now dressed in a shirt and tie. One street-tough, young woman was speaking her line about hope.   For the first time, she was wearing tailored clothing and heels. Two of our mischievous freshmen were basking in the limelight of respect for their project on global warming. Three other students were enjoying their newly experienced recognition as "*creative* kids." A female freshman proudly stood side by side with upper classmen. A regularly suspended student enjoyed the special role as camera operator, and shared this responsibility with a very talented and highly respected senior. Four talented youngsters graced the audience with their live musical performance. A trio of students proudly stood, center stage, next to a student who struggled socially. Finally, from behind the stage, came our student technician. Two other students humbly manned their stations on lights.

At the conclusion of our program, a well respected businessman and local CEO, Mr. Don Alexander, stated that he did not know what to expect. He explained that he did not know that he would experience so much and that he actually found himself buying into it. Mr. Alexander complimented our students when he told them that he could see that there was great hope for the future.

Reflection: Mary Ellen
Pilot #2 - It was a doozy!

February brought a strong wind, one that froze me to the bone. When the conditions are just right, my memory brings back that chill.

Roughly twenty students enrolled in the next run of the media literacy course. Astonishingly, six of the students chose to repeat the class from the previous semester. This brought a new challenge to the supervisors. They had to remain flexible and open-minded enough to keep the students in a forward movement of growth. We began by successfully including our *leader students* to demonstrate and assist the other students in the basics of teaming as well as the basics of the production process. This semester bore more plump fruit than the first, in terms of projects that were action based. In many ways, however, the negative elements that arose from our new mix of students were sadly ironic. The beauty of our efforts to empower and respect the individual student resulted in a sense of entitlement. This led to some destructive energies. Our efforts to treat and honor our students as young adults backfired. In a twist of pathetic irony, we were treated as if we were now hypocrites of our own philosophy, one that was designed to assure that the students would have their voices heard! Well, I never thought this implementation would be easy, but I did not imagine that the biggest hurdle to overcome would occur within my own classroom. I was creating all this with my students' best interests at heart and never anticipated the challenge that would follow. Before I tell you of what I now refer to as the dogged days of anarchy, let me share with you all the profoundly important topics and project outcomes that came from this second pilot.

Reflection: Mary Ellen and Swaz

The projects

I Pledge

Modeled after Ashton Kutcher and Demi Moore's YouTube film of various celebrities vowing to make a positive change for our country and for our world, the media literacy students collaborated with a sixth grade class to create their own <u>I Pledge</u>. This project was as far reaching as the multiple layers of impact that could be found by empowering the underclassmen to honor and use their voices. The high school students taught the middle school students how to use the software program, Windows Movie Maker. Then, they helped them to understand the positive impact that one person can have in the world. The students made a two minute commercial that was shown to our school audience during our morning announcements and at our Celebration of Learning Assembly. In addition, above and beyond the call of duty, the student directors provided the sixth graders with art supplies to create small paintings which would later be auctioned off for a benefit to support our local Children's Clinic. We thought that it was pretty brilliant. It led us to the next wonderful project.

The Children's Clinic

The Children's Clinic group organized the creation of 100, 6" x 6" paintings that would later be auctioned off at a fundraiser to benefit the Children's Clinic. The process was fully documented. When all was said and done, this team of students invited the dignitaries from the clinic and our school nurses to see a beautiful movie that captured the entire grassroots effort. The presentation was thoughtfully planned, invitations were sent, a continental breakfast was provided, original art pieces were unveiled, and the class of sixth graders was invited as special guests! It was a beautiful time. It was a time filled with gratitude and pride.

The Credit Union

The Credit Union team of students, who took the challenge offered by a neighboring banking business, was in for a difficult, yet rewarding, experience. The charge was to provide quality photographs for the new ATM machine that was recently constructed. The students thought that this task sounded easy enough. Meeting at the center of our little town at 6 a.m. wasn't exactly what they had anticipated as part of their job description; however, to ensure good lighting and ideal conditions for obtaining quality images, they found that an early arrival was absolutely necessary. The culmination of the students' work resulted in a slick, professional presentation to the credit union representatives. Brochures, PowerPoints, and enlarged photo selections were presented in state of the art formats by the team. The most impressive consideration was that the students surveyed sixty random people to ask them what specific visual image they thought would best capture our town of Adams, NY. They then proceeded to show images of the areas listed in the survey. The credit union representatives were impressed. On that day, we witnessed our youth being valued for their contributions and we understood that tomorrow's workforce may have great promise.

Women for Women

An all female team decided to speak out for women whose voices have been silenced. This team researched and showed images of women from Rwanda who had suffered the emotional and physical tortures of the genocide. Simply presented, the young advocates displayed photos and personal letters that were loaned to them by a member of the Women for Women international organization (www.womenforwomen.org). The students of the class were asked to walk by the display and then sign a pledge to help in any way that they could. They followed up with an intense multimedia presentation that drove the message home regarding the injustices that still exist in our world. We were all proud that this team took their work from the level of research-education to that of action.

Celebration of Learning (and discovery of addictions)

The anarchy began. One team was busy taking over the organizational reins to run an assembly program that was established a few years ago. Another team was working fiercely to produce what they held to be their best film yet. They had great hope of showcasing it at the Celebration of Learning Assembly. The unit of study focused on the national level and the topic they chose was drug abuse among teens. It was the thirst for an audience of their peers that fueled the intensity of commitment. This group was comprised primarily of our repeat student leaders. They were a group of highly intelligent, creative, and motivated learners. Their work was exceptional! Because their creation was so powerful, we felt the need to put on the breaks. We felt obligated to evaluate and consider the risks of showing such a strong, controversial piece to a general, high school audience. We feared that if the audience were not properly groomed to receive this extraordinary work, as it was intended, we would run the risk of them misinterpreting the film as glorifying drug use. Dialogue began in class and we indicated that we were considering the possibility of withholding the viewing of this film until the end of the course. We reasoned that a more mature, adult audience, would fully appreciate the intent of the movie. When we said that, the gloves came flying off and the students were postured for anarchy.

Journal entry: Mary Ellen - March 2009
Good God, I've created a monster!

Preface: I went to my school mailbox and found the anonymous letter. It was neatly typed with my name handwritten in pencil on the front. All three teachers received a copy of the letter. The letter was drafted as if it could have been used in a court of law. There was obviously more than one accuser, but there was clearly not to be a jury. We were already convicted. The charge was, guilty of hypocrisy. We shall suffer the highest punishment allowed by the judge. We were to give the students their way or face anarchy. The exact words were: "WE will go ahead with or without you." At first, we tried to appreciate the adolescent quality of it all. After all, they were simply being the creatures of rebellion that they were born to be at this age. Surely, they didn't mean to undermine our position and misinterpret our objections without regard for our feelings or thoughts on the matter. About three seconds later, when we were done rationalizing, we had to face the music. Feeling the weight of parental responsibility, I personally knew that I had a choice to enable them, hold them accountable, place restrictions over them for their own good, or ground them! After a few phone calls to my colleagues and a sleepless night, I realized that I needed to deliver a speech. The next morning, I was surprised that my body began to shake and I had to resist waves of emotion. I struggled to understand what my reaction was all about. Well, like a good parent, my heart was breaking, and I had to hold firm while I tried to teach my students the lessons that their young years had mercifully not yet taught them. I needed to protect them from their naïve intentions. Would their movie look like an anti-drug movie or a how-to tutorial? Their intentions were good, but the outcome could have been disastrous.

I delivered this speech with my two colleagues sitting on either side of me.

The speech

"Do not misinterpret kindness for weakness and do not misinterpret patience and compassion for vulnerability. This is not a room of anonymity, it is a room of open and honest communication. This is a prepared statement because whatever the outcome, there is much work to do to be prepared. I ended class yesterday saying that this discussion would be continued, because it was obvious that emotions were running high and there was a lack of closure. In the interim, I was reprimanded by one student, barked at by another student's demands, and had a lovely in-depth conversation with two of the students for another whole class period. I cried twice and had a meeting with my two colleagues in order to reflect upon what had transpired. Then, I received an anonymous three and a half page letter. It was filled with passion, commendable justifications, a few insults aimed at me, and a borderline threat to me and/or the course itself. I wish to summarize this way. The compromises that I offered were not enough, my respect for you and your work did not speak loudly enough. You demand your voice, which I want for you as well, but you demand it on your own terms and in the space, time, and conditions that you want. I am *one* voice that has labored over a decade of my life to formulate this course because I believe in you. I believe in *all* the young people that I have taught for 27 years, and *all* the young people that will be taught in the future. It is my judgment (based on experience), which was echoed in the anonymous letter, that there is a battle to be fought for a better way, and a better education system. That being said, there are also better ways to move forward rather than to jump to the front lines to engage in heavy battle. Study your opponent, strategically advance while you gain strength to conquer and then, win the war! The voice of youth is strong and powerful. It is immediate, urgent, passionate, and well-intended. After a long dialogue with my colleagues and support from our principal, we chose to re-open the *POTENTIAL* of the following two forums:

We will provide a health symposium, which was already offered, for a more mature and informed audience, or the Celebration of Learning Assembly in the auditorium. Either way, neither option is being promised at this point. There will be criteria and conditions to be met that will require one more round of approval. There will need to be the following: student signatures and parent signatures of those involved; proper preface for the audience; proper preface for the drug issue movie; disclaimers; copyright; and the re-working of the opening and the closing of the drug awareness film.

The presentation of the above-mentioned movie has not yet been solidified in terms of schedule and place. This puts a great burden on another team who is organizing the Celebration of Learning Assembly. This team has worked very hard and is under a lot of pressure. With this in mind, here is our plan of the day. [Three students were named.] Your immediate supervisor wishes for you to report to her for a five minute debriefing. You should resume work with your team to get your task done. Please provide me with access to the movie at that time. [Two other students were named.] Please meet with myself and your other supervisor in the computer room to work together on the summary of the Celebration of Learning. [Two more students were named.] Work on creating two posters please.

The rest of you may begin formulating loose ideas for unit two. Look up the schedule on our website and understand that we will end up with one less week for production, so take on an appropriate challenge for the time constraints.

All students, plan on prepping for Celebration of Learning on Monday-Wednesday, so that we are ready for Thursday. May we all celebrate our journey and its outcome. I wish you all the best of luck."

The speech was delivered and I was drained. We all got up and went about our business. One week later, at the Celebration of Learning Assembly, the students greeted everyone at the doors and handed them a colored piece of paper. The program was opened up with a speech that set the tone and spoke of the team's positive intent to deter "even one more person" from using drugs. Another student speaker shared devastating data related to drug abuse among our youth. During the speech, statistics from a middle school health survey, in which this very high school audience had previously participated, showed on the large screen on stage. As directed by the young, confident, female speaker, groups of students who held a particular color of paper stood to symbolize the statistics. The reality regarding the seriousness of the topic was well demonstrated. Next, the presenters invited our resident state trooper to the podium to speak on the dangers of drug abuse from his perspective. The audience was well-prepped and the six minute film was now unveiled. The audience responded positively to the powerfully directed and edited creation. The final speaker was the health teacher who had overseen the project. The students rose to the occasion, had their moment in the spotlight, and numerous teachers gave a positive comment as they departed. Our relationships, though somewhat fractured from this experience, did not detract from our ultimate goal. On that day, we all respected our new levels of commitment to this shared educational and human journey.

In the two months remaining of the school year, I think that students and teachers alike tried their best to forgive. One student wrote me a personal letter of apology, another came to speak to me with the intent of healing our rapport. I, too, initiated private conversations to close the gap. Whenever the opportunity afforded itself, I alluded to the broader lessons learned regarding freedom of speech, intrapersonal skills, and the like. Most of the anarchists graduated feeling well-deserved growing pains that propelled them into adulthood. Ultimately, I admired each of them for different reasons and continued to lick my own wounds of growth during the summer months.

Flash forward: The following year brought unexpected gifts of renewed rapport, increased *mutual* respect, and apologetic acknowledgments regarding the events that unfolded. Our hearts and minds were finally released with genuine forgiveness and closure.

Conclusion

What if each teacher honored students for their strengths?

What if teachers promoted global citizenship?

What if world peace was promoted like the advertising campaign to ban smoking in public places?

What if teachers were utilized for their strengths and not expected to do it all?

What if school buildings no longer existed?

What if each child had a personal computer and school was conducted on a bike, bus, or train?

What if?

CHAPTER 9

No chapter, to challenge left-brainers

No Kidding.

CHAPTER 10

The sunlight on the January icicles sparkled with the promise of a new beginning.

Agents of change needed now

"To everything there is a season,
and a time to every purpose under the heavens."
[Ecclesiastes 3:1]

Four letters

Dear students,

We deeply care about you. We care about what you can do and who you will become. We care about your goals and aspirations, about your future and the future of your children and your children's children. We want to give you the opportunity to utilize your potential to become the best that you can be. We want to capitalize on your strengths so that you may become productive members of today's world. We will offer you the forum to express yourselves through multimedia, to network with your peers, and to grow intellectually, socially, artistically, and emotionally. We will encourage you to create and present your work. We will give you a voice and a choice. This is your chance to shine, to rise to excellence, and to make the world a better place. Seize the day.

Françoise Piron

Dear Colleagues,

We all enter this profession as one person and exit it as another. I believe that the vast majority of us enter our careers sharing a common hope. We hope to prepare our students for the next steps in life and to arm them with the confidence and skills that they will need to be successful. We enter this profession seeing the whole child. We value that each of our colleagues is an important contributor to the psychological, intellectual, emotional, social, and spiritual attributes of each student. So, what happens over time that causes us to become primarily focused on our content areas? Think of your district and the professionals that make up your staff. What state mandates, delegation of funds, and public pressures create division? It is no secret that a hierarchy of content areas exists and is well-known by all in our profession. It is abundantly apparent at every faculty meeting and professional development event. We read of our pecking order in educational policy-making reports and in the news. Let's face it, we are postured to be at odds with one another. Territorialism, or worse, elitism, results in our inability to give students the educational experiences that they need and deserve. Our Hippocratic Oath, as educators, should read as follows: "I pledge to focus on that which will provide the highest quality educational experience for the individual student in order to best prepare her/him for the pursuit of a life filled with peace, health, happiness, and prosperity." With this oath as our guiding principle, one could be free to make more informed and purposeful decisions about curriculum and assessments. One could relax into the flexible variables that would allow us to let go of pre-defined territories. These territories have been so longstanding and obscurely delineated that we have forgotten why they were even created. If one kept the well-being of each student at the forefront of one's mind, one would be more willing to accept one's own limitations and strengths. We would be courageous enough to redefine each person's contributing role as content specialist, facilitator, counselor, lesson planner, presenter, or assessor. Who decided that *we*, as teachers, must be good at everything?

After all, does a doctor have to be a good accountant, surgeon, technician, and family counselor? Doctors are highly specialized to best serve their patients. My dear colleagues, we are at odds with one another because the Industrial Age education model, under which we still work, demands that we enter our 21st century professions with 19th century restrictions. No wonder we find ourselves jostling to prove whose content area is most important or whose space deserves the latest, state of the art updates. No wonder we banter over whose style of teaching is in vogue. After 28 years of teaching, I still see professional jealousy and division. Allowing division and conflict to permeate our schools undermines our purpose at the expense of our dignity! In the end, no matter how one cuts it, the root cause of discontent lies in the fear-filled and insecure hearts of those who were misled into thinking that superiority must be accomplished in order for one's own interests to be realized. Has history not taught us that this is a lie? What a shame, what a waste. My friends, rebuke the division and embrace our common goals. Empower one another. Please, fellow colleagues, open your minds and hearts. Let down your wall and let go of pride and insecurity so that we can truly unite and move forward into a hopeful time, an educational renaissance. I ask you the following: in the privacy of these pages that you now read on your own terms, are you willing to set aside past teaching styles for the sake of what our students need in the 21st century? Are you humble enough to let go of the identity and control of what it once meant to be *the* teacher of the classroom? Are you flexible enough (and not damaged by the cycle of new mandates, jargon, and strategies) to let go of your control? Are you ready to join a community of educators who respect one another's strengths and weaknesses in order to maximize what we can model for our youth? Are you ready to embrace change as our constant and celebrate the most exciting times in the history of education as it relates to global citizenry? If you are willing, then I say, Godspeed *and fasten* your seatbelts. It's surely going to be one hell of a ride!

Mary Ellen Shevalier

Dear educational leaders, Boards of Education, union leaders, business administrators, and state governors,

Are you ready to re-acquaint yourselves with innocence and let your painfully earned status be used to contribute to the truth of what our world needs now? Your support is absolutely essential and *is* the single most important element that can either propel us forward or stifle our hopes and dreams. We need you to turn over every stone to provide incentives and to help us to accept the risks associated with change. What will it cost? Surely, it will not cost us nearly as much as turning a blind eye or a deafening ear. Pretend *we* are your students. Do for us what you want us to do for them. Believe in us, encourage us, empower and reward us. Educators are dying to be heard. We are weary of begging to be given the permission, support, and resources to be creative, intelligent, and resourceful professionals. We are tired of the countless hoops that we have to maneuver and jump through in order to embrace change. We wish for your blessing to jump freely through the hoops of progress, so that we may reach our students with the gifts which are uniquely ours.

Mary Ellen Shevalier

The Re-education of America

Dear students,

I write to you for three reasons: to apologize to you, to encourage you, and to ask you for your help.

First, may I apologize for not being courageous enough or fast enough to really make the difference in creating a more meaningful education for you. I also must own my part in not valuing your individuality as much as I could have. True, I have tried my best to help students discover themselves through my curriculum, the arts, but I am as guilty as the next teacher for being territorial, thinking that my way was the right way, and for not promoting interdisciplinary differentiation sooner. As I have matured in years and have benefited from life's lessons, I now know the difference. I see you, each one of you, and I want to guide each of you to achieve in accordance with your potential. What I mean to say is, although I started out as an art teacher, I have now become a teacher of children. I honor you for your various gifts and I accept your various weaknesses. I wish I had promoted this sooner and with more vigor. Now that I have that off my chest, I would like to acknowledge your power and capacity to move forward in the age of 21st century learning. You deserve all the benefits inherent in our new and ever-changing world. Technology has freed you to gather information as you wish. It has also given you a world-wide audience eager to listen and appreciate you for who you are. I want you to understand that although teachers can be wonderful guides to expedite your journey and to help you to connect the dots along the way, they cannot learn *for* you. In order to become who you are meant to be, it is up to you to motivate, inquire, and create. If you would like a better educational system that fosters learning and if you accept the notion that teachers have the training, expertise, and your best interest at heart, then just encourage them to enter your world. You see, we are in a time of great transition and we could use your assistance in building confidence in areas of new technology and thought. Help us to let go of old methods that serve to isolate and stifle us. Help us to understand that your world is all about teams: construction workers, doctors, law firms, musicians, scientists, writers, day care, lawn care, and every other care in the world. Help us to understand that, not unlike us, you are yearning for individual choice and creative problem solving. Help us to remember that experiences do not become knowledge until we are given a chance to be heard, to reflect, and to utilize. Help us to understand what author Kahlil Gibran wrote in <u>The Prophet</u>, "You may give them your love but not your thoughts, for they have thoughts of their own. You may house their bodies, but not their souls, for their souls dwell in the house of tomorrow, which you cannot visit, not even in your dreams." Be gentle with us during this transition so that we may humbly let go. Finally, as you take what you rightfully deserve, remember above all that none of us is simply entitled. We must earn our rights, and be thankful for the many that have paid a price before us so that we may have an opportunity to build. Together, with mutual respect and a common goal to better our own lives, our country and our world, let us move forward in kindness and patience.

Mary Ellen Shevalier

World Class

Journal entry: Mary Ellen - Aug. 1, 2009
Hitting home

We see it all over the news, tsunamis, hurricanes, flash floods, and murders. Yet, somehow, if it doesn't hit our neighborhoods we immunize ourselves, anesthetize ourselves. It is easier that way. It is too much to take it all in.

As I entered little town, USA, for the calling hours of Lance Jeremy Lasher, Marine Corps, my eyes filled with water as my heart expanded to invite the pain shared by so many who knew or didn't know this fallen soldier. My lower lip opened slightly as I saw the rural routes speckled with red, white, and blue. Sound escaped these same lips as I drove past curtains of American flags that waved to each of us from virtually every house along Main Street. The theater marquee as well as the VFW and fire hall in the little town of Oneida, NY, heralded Marine Lasher's name as if to hail all the angels to hover. Only two more days until the funeral was over. This would complete the escort home that his brother, and fellow Marine, had begun in Afghanistan. I arrived at the funeral home and was greeted with a hug from my brother, a former Marine. He was there in support of his significant other, the mother-in-law of the fallen soldier.

I saw a stream of Marines, dressed in full military uniform, descend down the stairs and into Jeremy's room to await the arrival of the wife, the mother, and the siblings of our hero. When the double doors opened, the flag-covered coffin held center stage on the altar of sacrifice that was flanked by candle-like figures of Marines, standing perfectly still and shining brightly. As I made my way down the family line, my brother came to my side to identify our relation. I moved from the deceased soldier's sister to his civilian-clad Marine brother, two more brothers, spouses, step-father, mother, and then, finally, his wife. I paused to hug and hold, sometimes comforting and other times being comforted while expressing the feelings in my heart. The words came out in a tearful stream at first, but by the time I reached Jeremy's wife, my words became broken, louder, and crackled. Choking, I said, "Thank you for the sacrifice that you and your family have made for me and our country. I will continue to pray for you and your family."

When I reached the other side of Jeremy's casket, whispering thank you to the Marines and God, I hugged Jeremy's mother-in-law and my brother. I will never hear of another fallen soldier and not acknowledge and be thankful for the personal loss and sacrifice of his or her family. My brother's eyes watered as he willed himself to stay strong. We hugged and each said, "I love you." Later, standing under our umbrellas, the sidewalk now lined with firefighters and volunteers holding American flags, my nieces, nephew, and I huddled to avoid the raindrops. Then, my niece said, "Through our father's choice, our family is blended with this family. God has made us a family, and that's that. We will be there for them." Her words stamped another imprint on my psyche and soul. My niece added, "If we could all understand that we ARE all family, as God intended, we wouldn't be at a soldier's funeral today." On the way home, my spirit adopted what my mind refused to ponder for too long. Every family, from every generation, from every culture who has suffered a loss due to war, is connected. Then, almost shamefully, my thoughts flooded back to my course, "I am a Citizen of the World." We must teach one another to celebrate our diversity, to embrace our differences, and to work through our dysfunctions as the people that we are, *a family*.

We must teach this.
We must teach peace.

World Peace will come

It will come from the hearts of our children.

Peace will flow from one child
 to another like a natural brook,
sometimes bubbling and sometimes trickling,
but always flowing
past all the rocks of old hatred,
broken twigs of fear and the moss
 of apathy that grows only in the shadows of
a closed heart.

World peace will come.
It will come when we teach our children
the commonalities of the human race,
when we teach them about the universality
of our needs to express ourselves, to be
heard and loved.

World Peace will come.

EPILOGUE: So, now what?

You have read the many stories and anecdotes that pepper this book. You have followed our journey from an idea to a new course and you understand the need for change. You believe in schools that are better suited for their students and you are eager to take part in the development of a new education system. You understand that the time is NOW and that we are at a major crossroad. Now what? What should YOU do about it? Perhaps you can start a grassroots movement in your school and create a professional learning community whereby you invite students and staff to collaborate on a project to make your school a better place for a better world. At South Jefferson Central School we started exactly that. With the help of our district technology leader, RaeAnn Thomas, we created a forum entitled "reinventED". It is a grassroots collaborative forum that all stakeholders may join. We meet a few times a year and communicate regularly via technology to inspire one another, discuss ideas, brain*stream* solutions and see what we can do to move forward.

For more information, please visit our wiki at: http://sjcsreinvented.pbworks.com.

Just one year after reinventED's debut, our technology leader created another site to attract more teachers. She did so by setting it up specifically to share and to use as a project that credits us with professional development hours. It is a brilliant and simple site called "collaboration station." It invites all teachers, in the district and beyond, to participate and share ideas and/or expertise.

The site is maintained by Ms. Thomas, who encourages participation by sending out a few small tasks each month.

May you create a forum that fits your needs and that helps you to develop the tools necessary to bring your school into the 21st century.

Remember who **we*** are. **We*** are the change, **we*** are the answer.

REFERENCES:

Here are other resources that may add insight to each chapter's general theme on educational reform.

Chapter 1: Who else out there wants educational reform?

Educational organizations whose goal is to reform education:

NYSCATE (The New York State Association for Computers and Technologies in Education), is a non-profit, professional organization representing more than 2,000 technology using educators and administrators in New York State. NYSCATE is an affiliate of the International Society for Technology in Education (ISTE), and cooperates with such partners as the New York State Education Department, state and national educational organizations, private sector corporations, and publishers to further the use of technology in our schools. NYSCATE is involved in helping define statewide policy regarding the use of technologies in education.

Mission: NYSCATE is an organization of dedicated technology using educators, committed to transforming teaching and learning, in order to provide our children with an education that prepares them to live satisfying and productive lives.

Link: http://www.nyscate.org/aboutus.cfm

ISTE

The International Society for Technology in Education is the trusted source for professional development, knowledge generation, advocacy, and leadership for innovation.

Mission: ISTE advances excellence in learning and teaching through innovative and effective uses of technology.

Membership: ISTE members include more than 20,000 individuals, 80 regional and international affiliate organizations, and 61 corporations.

With its international network of affiliates, ISTE represents more than 100,000 education leaders and emerging leaders throughout the world.

Link:
http://www.iste.org/AM/Template.cfm?Section=About_ISTE

U.S. Department of Education

Mission: Congress established the U.S. Department of Education (ED) on May 4, 1980, in the Department of Education Organization Act (Public Law 96-88 of October 1979). Under this law, ED's mission is to:

- Strengthen the Federal commitment to assuring access to equal educational opportunity for every individual;
- Supplement and complement the efforts of states, the local school systems and other instrumentalities of the states, the private sector, public and private nonprofit educational research institutions, community-based organizations, parents,

and students to improve the quality of education;

- Encourage the increased involvement of the public, parents, and students in Federal education programs;
- Promote improvements in the quality and usefulness of education through Federally supported research, evaluation, and sharing of information;
- Improve the coordination of Federal education programs;
- Improve the management of Federal education activities; and
- Increase the accountability of Federal education programs to the President, the Congress, and the public.

ED was created in 1980 by combining offices from several federal agencies. ED's mission is to promote student achievement and preparation for global competitiveness by fostering educational excellence and ensuring equal access. ED's 4,200 employees and $68.6 billion budget are dedicated to:

- Establishing policies on federal financial aid for education, and distributing as well as monitoring those funds.
- Collecting data on America's schools and disseminating research
- Focusing national attention on key educational issues.
- Prohibiting discrimination and ensuring equal access to education.
- Link: http://www.ed.gov/about/overview/mission/mission.html

211

ASCD (formerly the Association for Supervision and Curriculum Development) Founded in 1943, is an educational leadership organization dedicated to advancing best practices and policies for the success of each learner. Our 160,000 members in 148 countries are professional educators from all levels and subject areas––superintendents, supervisors, principals, teachers, professors of education, and school board members.

Link: http://www.ascd.org/about-ascd.aspx

UNESCO (United Nations Educational, Scientific and Cultural Organization)
Founded on 16 November 1945. For this specialized United Nations agency, it is not enough to build classrooms in devastated countries or to publish scientific breakthroughs. This organization intends a far more ambitious goal: to build peace in the minds of men.
Mission: The mission of the UNESCO Education Sector is to:

- Provide international leadership to create learning societies with educational opportunities for all populations.
- Provide expertise and foster partnerships to strengthen national educational leadership and the capacity of countries to offer quality education for all.
- Work as an intellectual leader, an honest broker and clearinghouse for ideas, propelling both countries and

the international community to accelerate progress towards these goals.

- Facilitate the development of partnerships and monitor progress; in particular by publishing an annual report that tracks the achievements of countries and the international community towards the achievement of quality education for all.

Links:
http://www.efareport.unesco.org

http://www.unesco.org/en/education/about-us/mission

http://portal.unesco.org/en/ev.ph

http://www.unesco.org/en/efa-international-coordination/the-efa-movement/efa-goals

Chapter 2: Project-Based Learning

1. "Therefore, it stands to reason that altering our experiences will alter our brain. This is a simple but profound syllogism: Our brain is involved in all we do, our brain changes from experience; therefore our experiences at school will change our brain in some way. Instead of narrowing the discussion about brain research in education to dendrites and axons, a contemporary discussion would include a wider array of topics. Brain-based education says that we use evidence from all disciplines to enhance the brains of students."

Jensen, Eric P. (Feb. 2008). A Fresh Look at Brain-Based Education, Phi Delta Kappan,V89-N6, p.412 www.pdkintl.org

2. "A mind map is a visualization of thought. Knowledge is not linear. All kinds of things radiate from your head when you have an idea. It is like an explosion, a supernova. That's the thought process that a mind map helps to capture. The mind really works in multiple thoughts and directions at the same time-radiant thinking, thinking from an image at the centre and radiating outward. The brain is self-organizing. It's designed to organize and manage knowledge. It has astonishing power to do that. It is in part a blank slate."

Dearlove and Crainer, (Dec 2007). Management Mentors on Tony Buzan and Mind Mapping, http://www.management-issues.com/2007/12/4/mentors/tony-buzan-on-mind-mapping .asp

3. "Stephen Covey, an internationally recognized leadership specialist and the author of *The 7 Habits of Highly Effective People* and *The 8th Habit,* points to the need for all individuals, regardless of age, to find purpose in their lives. Whether discussing the curriculum for a child or the needs of an adult learner, Covey encourages the development of the whole person."

"Daniel Pink (added): At a very significant level of who we are, we know that when we focus on a single area of anything we are grossly overlooking other areas of significance.

Twentieth-century thinking looked for the one right answer, one right program, one right piece of legislation- a silver-bullet mentality that does not exist. It never has and certainly in the complex work of the 21st century never will."

McCaw, Donna S. (Feb. 2007). Dangerous Intersection Ahead, The School Administrator, pp. 1 & 4

http://www.aasa.org/content.aspx?id=1896

4." Routines and right answers are commodities. They are essentially free, anybody can do them, therefore they have zero or almost zero economic value. Whereas the ability to think, being able to be creative, to empathize with others, to tell a story, to listen to other people's story; being adept at design, at connecting the dots, at recognizing patterns, at pursuing a life of purpose- those are not just the things that are going to enrich the young people as human beings, but those are the types of things that our children are going to be doing for a living. So there is a sort of double whammy flaw in the routines and right answers obsession being used right now by many public school regimes."

Pink, Daniel, American Association of School Administrators-Publications-Daniel Pink: A whole New Mind

http://www.aasa.org/search.aspx?query=Daniel +Pink

5. "The member high schools emphasized project-based learning, in which standards are embedded in an integrated curriculum. Students

create projects that meet various standards or parts of standards by creating their own "performance packages" built around Minnesota's High Standards Profiles of Learning. All students achieve the state standards by creating products that indicate a high level of understanding, not by passing knowledge-based tests. Usually the projects conclude with a performance or yield a product that can be assessed for the kind of lifelong learning skills exhibited by the student and can be measured against the inquiry-based content standards the student has made use of in the final product or performance."

Newell, Ronald J. (2002) A Different Look at Accountability: The EdVisions Approach, Phi Delta Kappan, November 2002, Vol. 84, N3, p 209.

www.pdkintl.org

6. "The mediation of the mind happens when an individual is taught the what, the why, and the how. Just as a computer has a programmer for the software, so a student has individuals who help develop the mind. Reuven Feuerstein studied under Jean Piaget and asked him how he accounted for individual differences. Piaget, a biologist, was more interested in accommodation and assimilation. Feurerstein believed that when a caring adult intervened using mediation, significant learning occurred."

Ruby K. Payne, Ph.D., founder of aha. Dr. Payne is the author of numerous books, including *A Framework for Understanding Poverty* (more than 1 million copies sold) and *Bridges Out of Poverty*.

www.ahaprocess.com

7. "Creativity is the strongest example of the dynamic nature of intelligence, and it can call on all areas of our minds and being."

Robinson, Sir Ken, (2009) The Element, Viking Penguin Group, (USA)Incorporated., 375 Hudson St. N.Y.,N.Y., Pg 70

Chapter 3: Educational Policy; its seduction and failure

1. "Test-Driven accountability is now the norm in public schools, a result of the No Child Left Behind (NCLB) Act, which is the culmination of 15 years of standards-based reform. Many state and local officials believe that this relevance on tests is too narrow a measure of educational achievement, but NCLB has directed greater attention to low-achieving students and intensified efforts to improve persistently low-performing schools." "...However, under NCLB, student achievement is equated with the proportion of students who are scoring at the proficient level on the state tests, and states have adopted various approaches in their testing programs, such as the use of confidence intervals, that result in more test scores being counted as proficient. In addition, some national studies support our survey findings of increased student achievement, while others do not."

Jennings, Jack and Rentner, Diane Stark, (Oct.

2006). Ten Big Effects of the No Child Left Behind Act on Public Schools. Phi Delta Kappan, Vol.88-N2, p.110

www.pdkintl.org

2. "For example, even Education Week, known for its relentless advocacy of the standards-and-testing agenda, has acknowledged that there is "virtually unanimous agreement among experts that no single measure should decide a student's academic fate." *   This is certainly true. The prestigious National Research Council came to that conclusion **as have most other professional organizations (e.g., the American Educational Research Association and the American Psychological Association), the generally pro-testing American Federation of Teachers, and even the companies that manufacture and sell the tests.   To make students repeat a grade or to deny them diplomas on the basis of a single exam is unconscionable. Yet, at this writing, about half of the states are either doing so or planning to do so."
Kohn, Alfie, (Jan. 2001) , Fighting the Tests, A Practical Guide to Rescuing Our Schools, Phi Delta Kappan,Vol.82-N5, p.352

*Lynn Olson, "Worries of a Standards 'Backlash' Grow," Education Week, 5 April 2000, p. 12.

**Jay P. Heubert and Robert M. Hauser, eds., High Stakes: Testing for Tracking, Promotion, and Graduation (Washington, D. C.: National Academy Press, 1999).

www.pdkintl.org

3. (On NCLB. Is it working?) "No, it isn't, according to leaders in the science of testing. Scores always rise when you put high stakes on a particular test, whether or not students actually know more. This phenomenon even has a name: Campbell's Law."

Jehlen, Alain. (2009), "Is NCLB Working? The Scientifically-based answer." neatoday, V27.N.4 pp. 30-31

Chapter 4: It's not all about us. The universality of metacognition

1. "Many teachers would describe metacognition, quite acceptable, as "thinking about thinking." But I would propose a more precise definition: Metacognition is the monitoring and control of thought."

Martinez, Martin, (May 2006). What Is Metacognition? Phi Delta Kappan, Vol.87-N9, p.696

2. "The generality of some functions is stated plainly by Ann Brown in a seminal article on metacognition. 'The skills of metacognition do appear to have recognizable counterparts in real-world, everyday-life situations'. Checking the results of an operation against certain criteria of effectiveness, economy, and commonsense reality is a metacognitive skill applicable whether the task under consideration is solving a math problem, memorizing a prose passage, following

a recipe, or assembling an automobile. Self-interrogation concerning the state of one's own knowledge during problem solving is an essential skill in a wide variety of situations, those of the laboratory, the school, or everyday life."*

Martinez, Martin, (May 2006).What Is Metacognition? Phi Delta Kappan,Vol.87-N9, p.696

* Ann L. Brown, "Knowing When, where and How to Remember is A Problem of Metacognition: in Robert Glaser, ed., Advances in Instructional Psychology, vol. 1 (Hillsdale, N.J.: Erlbaum, 1978). P.80

www.pdkintl.org

3. "Metacognition has to do with the active monitoring and regulation of cognitive processes. It represents the "executive control" system that many cognitive theorists have included in their theories (e.g., Miller, Newell & Simon, Schoenfeld). Metacognitive processes are central to planning, problem-solving, evaluation and many aspects of language learning.
Vaidya, Sheila R., (1999) Definition of Metacognition, Education, Vol, 120.

4. Metacognition refers to higher order thinking which involves active control over the cognitive processes engaged in learning. Activities such as: planning how to approach a given learning task, monitoring comprehension, and evaluation progress toward the completion of a task are metacognitive in nature.

Livingston, Jennifer A. (1997), Metacognition: An Overview

http://www.gse.buffalo.edu/fas/shuell/cep564/Metacog.htm

5. "Novice learners don't stop to evaluate their comprehension of the material. They generally don't examine the quality of their work or stop to make revisions as they go along. Satisfied with just scratching the surface, novice learners don't attempt to examine a problem in depth. They don't make connections or see the relevance of the material in their lives. Expert learners are "more aware than novices of when they need to check of errors, why they fail to comprehend, and how they need to redirect their efforts."

Ertmer, P.A. & Newby, T.J., (1996). The expert learner: strategic, self-regulated, and reflective. Instructional Science 21: 1-24. Netherlands: Kluwer Academic Publishers

http://coe.sdsu.edu/eet/Articles/metacognition/start.htm

6. "When people are in the zone, they align naturally with a way of thinking that works best for them. I believe this is the reason that time seems to take on a new dimension when you are in the zone. It comes from a level of effortlessness that allows for such full immersion that you simply don't "feel" time the same way. This effortlessness has a direct relationship to thinking styles. When people use a thinking style completely natural to them, everything comes more easily."

World Class

Robinson, Sir Ken, (2009) The Element, Viking Penguin Group, (USA) Incorporated, 375 Hudson St. N.Y.,N.Y.p. 96

7. Partnership for 21stcentury Skills (www.21stcenturyskills.org):
Core Subjects and 21st Century Themes

Mastery of core subjects and 21st century themes is essential for students in the 21st century. Core subjects include:

- English, reading or language arts
- World languages
- Arts
- Mathematics
- Economics
- Science
- Geography
- History
- Government and Civics

In addition to these subjects, we believe schools must move beyond a focus on basic competency in core subjects to promoting understanding of academic content at much higher levels by weaving **21st century interdisciplinary themes** into core subjects:

- **Global awareness**
- **Financial, economic, business and entrepreneurial literacy**
- **Civic literacy**

- **Health literacy**
- **Environmental literacy**

Chapter 5:   The state of the classroom; a microcosm of the state of our country and of the world.

1. "Goleman (1995, 1998) concluded that emotional intelligence is the ability to motivate oneself and persist in the face of frustrations. Moreover, it includes the ability to control impulses, delay gratification, regulate one's moods, and keep distress from swamping the ability to think, empathize, and hope.   This suggests that school success may be adversely affected by emotional intelligence.   School performance may rise and fall more due to emotional management or mismanagement within the culture than the mere academic success or process improvements of the organization. It may be reasonable to argue that learning organizations can use a dose of emotional intelligence to facilitate success."

Calderin, Dr. Roberto, (2007), Ensemble Leadership: The role of emotional intelligence in assembling the resident talent of an organization,

SAANYS Journal, Vol. 36, N.2, p. 3

2."Students who are motivated to complete a task only to avoid consequences or to earn a certain grade rarely exert more than the minimum effort necessary to meet their goal. And, when students are focused on comparing themselves with their classmates, rather than on mastering skills at their own rate, they are more easily discouraged and their intrinsic motivation to learn may actually decrease. Brooks et al. (1998) observe that while external rewards sustain productivity, they "decrease interest in the task, thereby diminishing the likelihood that the task will be continued in the future." (p. 26)

3. "It should be noted here that some researchers object to describing student motivation as either intrinsic or extrinsic. Sternberg and Lubart (as cited in Strong, Silver, & Robinson, 1995) for example, argue that this division is too simple to reflect the many complex and interrelated factors that influence students' motivation to succeed in school. They point out that most successful people are motivated by both internal and external factors, and suggest that educators build on both types when working to engage students more fully in school."

Brewster, Cori & Fager, Jennifer, (2000) Increasing Student Engagement and Motivation: From Time-on-Task to Homework, Motivation: What does the Research Say, Northwest Regional Educational Laboratory, pp. 4-5

http://www.nwrel.ort/request/oct00/textonly.html

4. Strategies for Motivating Students
- Become a role model for student interest
- Get to know your students
- Use examples freely

- Use a variety of student-active teaching activities.
- Set realistic performance goals
- Place appropriate emphasis on testing and grading.
- Be free with praise and constructive in criticism.
- Give students as much control over their own education as possible.

Ken Bain, What the Best College Teachers Do, Harvard University Press, 2004, pages 32-42

Linda Nilson, Teaching At its Best: A Research-Based Resource for College Instructors, 2nd edition Anker Publishing, 2003, pages 41-44

Matt DeLong and Dale Winter, Learning to Teaching and Teaching to Learn Mathematics: Resources for Professional Development, Mathematical Association of America, 2002, pp 159-168

5. "Katz (1988) provides a useful conceptualization of learning when she asserts that learning consists of four interrelated types: knowledge (acquiring information), skill (the ability to demonstrate a particular behavioral repertoire), feelings (the emotions connected with the learning), and dispositions ("habits of mind" that become internalized, such as curiosity or persistence). In any given learning situation, all four co-exist and are equally important."

Katz, L.G. (1988). Early childhood education: What research tells us. Bloomington, IN: Phi Delta Kappa, as reprinted in: Jalongo, Mary Renck, Childhood Education: Beyond Benchmarks and Scores: Reasserting the Role of Motivation (2007) p 2

6. "Elkhonon Goldberg, writing in The Wisdom Paradox in 2005, suggest that the major capacity question a brain must ask whenever it confronts a challenge is "Have I confronted this problem before?" He argues that in most people, the right hemisphere lobes process novel challenges and develop creative solutions, and the left hemisphere lobes process familiar challenges and execute established routines."

Sylwester, Robert, (Dec., 2006) Cognitive Neuroscience Discoveries and Educational Practices, The School Administrator

7. "Schools are run by older people who know the answers, and the students are young people who want to explore the challenges. Schools thus often teach students the answers to questions they haven't yet asked, that don't engage them emotionally. Students obviously need to master basic skills and their cultural heritage, but the challenge for educators is to create the right mix of didactic instruction and creative student exploration-and to reflect this mix in standards and assessment programs."

Sylwester, Robert, (Dec., 2006) Cognitive Neuroscience Discoveries and Educational Practices,The School Administrator

8."Learn from them and you will see the new culture of high performance work, the twenty-first century schools and colleges, the innovative corporation, a more open family, and a democracy where citizens are engaged, and perhaps even the new, networked society."

Tapscott, Don (2009), GrownUp Digital, How the Net Generation is Changing Your World. McGraw Hill Co., New York: p. 13

Chapter 6: The Layout: collaboration is key!

1. "If schools want to enhance their organizational capacity to boost student learning, they should work on building a professional community that is characterized by shared learning, they should work on building a professional community that is characterized by shared purpose, collaborative activity, and collective responsibility among staff"

 Newmann F. & Wehlage, G. (1995) Successful school restructuring: A report to the public and educators by the Center for Restructuring Schools, Madison, WE: University of Wisconsin, p.37

2. "What separates a learning community from an ordinary school is its collective commitment to guiding principles that articulate what the people in the school believe and what they seek to create."

DuFour, R. & Eaker, R. (1998) Professional Learning Communities at Work, Best Practices for Enhancing Student Achievement, National Educational Service, Bloomington, Indiana, p.25

3. "Professional teachers emphasize learning rather than teaching. The focus of traditional schools is teaching; the focus of the professional learning community is student learning. The difference is much more than semantics. It represents a fundamental shift in the teacher-student relationship....Teachers in professional learning communities recognize that teaching has not occurred until learning has occurred, and they act accordingly.

    DuFour, R. & Eaker, R. (1998) Professional Learning Communities at Work, Best Practices for Enhancing Student Achievement, National Educational Service, Bloomington, Indiana, p.216

4. "A successful face-to face team is more than just collectively intelligent. It makes everyone work harder, think smarter and reach better conclusions than they would have on their own."
    Surowiecki, J. (2004), The Wisdom of crowds, New York Doubleday. 1745 Broadway, New York NY 10019

5. "Unlike typical staff development, learning communities encourage teachers to recognize and share the best of what they already know. This approach insists on the fundamental elements that workshops routinely ignore: collective follow-up, assessment, and adjustment of instruction."
    Schmoker, M. (2006) Results Now, ASCD, Virginia, USA, p.109

6. "When employers are asked what qualities will best prepare students for the modern workplace,

they often mention teamwork- the ability to cooperate and communicate with others to reach common goals. As Brown points out, 'Group effectiveness skills, including interpersonal communication, negotiation, and teamwork, are essential in today's diverse classroom and work-place.' (2001, p.1)"

Brown, B. L., (2001) Group effectiveness in the classroom and workplace (Practice application brief No. 15). Columbus, OH: Center on Educational Training for Employment. As cited in; Holloway, John, H., (Dec 2003-Jan. 2004) Research Link, Student Teamwork, Educational Leadership, Vol. 61, N. 4,p.91

7. "Gillies and Ashman (1998) found that students who were trained in cooperative group processes worked together better and were more committed to their group than were students who did not receive such training."

Gillies, R. M., & Ashman, A. (1998). Behavior and interactions of children in cooperative groups in lower and middle elementary grades., Journal of Educational Psychology, 90, pp. 746-757 as cited in; Holloway, John, H., (Dec 2003-Jan. 2004) Research Link, Student Teamwork, Educational Leadership, Vol. 61, N. 4,p.91

8. "Lopata, Miller, and Miller (2003) found that teachers who participated in professional development for cooperative learning were more likely to engage students in activities requiring team-work skills. These researchers found that to be successful, this professional development must focus on the collaborative components of

cooperative learning- specifically, positive interdependence, face-to-face interaction, and group process."

Holloway, John, H., (Dec 2003-Jan. 2004) Research Link, Student Teamwork, Educational Leadership, Vol. 61, N. 4,p.92

Chapter 7: The 4 "P's". Process, Proposal, Product, Presentation

1. "Internal control psychology is based upon the belief that people are internal, not externally, motivated. Powerful instructions that are built into our genetic structure drive our behavior to the outside world, including all rewards and punishment, only provides us with information. It does not *make* us do anything...students who are subjected to rewards and punishment over an extended period see themselves as "Out of control"- people whose success or failure is attributable to forces outside of themselves. They become irresponsible."

Sullo, Bob, (2007), Activating the Desire to Learn, Association for Supervision and Curriculum Development, Alexandria, Virginia, p.7

2. "William Glasser's (1998) choice theory, a biological theory that suggests we are born with specific need that we are genetically instructed to satisfy. All of our behavior represents our best attempt at any moment to satisfy our basic needs or genetic instructions. In addition to the

physical need for survival, we have four basic psychological needs that must be satisfied to be emotionally healthy: Belonging or connecting, Power or competence, Freedom, Fun."

Glasser, W. (1990) The quality school: Managing students without coercion., New York: Perennial Library as cited in: Sullo, Bob, (2007) Activating the Desire to Learn, Association for Supervision and Curriculum Development, Alexandria, Virginia, P.8

3. "Having students consciously and regularly self-evaluate is one characteristic of a classroom utilizing internal control psychology."

Sullo, Bob, (2007) Activating the Desire to Learn, Association for Supervision and Curriculum Development, Alexandria, Virginia, P.13

4. "Led by Partnership for 21st century Skills (www.21stcenturyskills.org). The four companies possessed several hundred employers, asking them to "articulate the skill sets that new entrants (into the workforce) need to succeed." When employers were asked to rank nine basic skills (including reading comprehension, math, and science) and 11 applied skills (such as critical thinking) in order of their importance for success in the workplace, the few identified as the most important for graduates from every level were: 1) professionalism/work ethic; 2) teamwork/collaboration: 3) oral communication; and 4) critical thinking/problem solving."

Fletcher, Geoffrey H., (2007) , An Eye on the Future, The Journal, vol 32, N. 7, p. 26 www.thejournal.com

5. "...something I got from my friend Ramalinga Raju from Satyam, the Indian company. We decided that the greatest economic competition in the world going forward is not going to be between countries and countries. And it's not going to be between companies and companies. The greatest economic competition going forward is going to be between you and your own imagination. Your ability to act on your imagination is going to be so decisive in driving your future and the standard of living in your country. So the school, the state, the country that empowers, nurtures, enables imagination among its students and citizens, that's who's going to be the winner."

The School Administrator, (2008) A discussion with author Daniel Pink on curiosity, passion and the politics of school reform in the global marketplace, featuring Thomas Friedman on Education in the 'Flat World'.

http://www.aasa.org/publications/saarticledetail.cfm?

7. "How does emotional intelligence fit into the academic curriculum? There are many kinds of learning that go on in school. And there's the explicit curriculum—math, language, the content. And there's the implicit curriculum—learning how to get along with other people, learning how to

motivate yourself, learning how to persist, how to resist temptation and stay fixed on a goal, how to work together toward a common goal. These implicit lessons actually over the course of life I believe turn out to be even more important than whether you know how to do quadratic equations."

Goleman, Daniel (2/22/2001) A View on Emotional Intelligence, Edutopia

http://www.edutopia.org/daniel-goleman-emotional-intelligence#graph5

8."...helpful to list the key instructional moves under the three broad categories of teaching types derived from Adler (1982) in *The Paideia Proposal*: didactic (or direct) instruction, coaching of skills, and facilitation (maieutics, as he terms it)."

Wiggins, Grant and McTighe Jay, (1998) Understanding by Design, Association for Supervision and Curriculum Development, Alexandria, Virginia, p.159

Chapter 8 Teaming: fundamental lessons for global citizenship

1. "The 2006 PISA science assessment explores the relevance and importance that students attach to scientific issues in questions posed alongside those that test their cognitive abilities. Moreover, the ALL survey has experimented with assessing individuals' ability to co-operate with

others, working in teams, although so far it has been difficult to translate this into a workable assessment within an international survey."

THE DEFINITION AND SELECTION OF KEY COMPETENCIES, Executive Summary, DeSeCo Project, www.oecd.org/edu/statistics/deseco, www.deseco.admin.ch

2. "Marzano's New Taxonomy is made up of three systems and the Knowledge Domain, all of which are important for thinking and learning. The three systems are the Self-System, the Metacognitive System, and the Cognitive System. When faced with the option of starting a new task, the Self-System decides whether to continue the current behavior or engage in the new activity; the Metacognitive System sets goals and keeps track of how well they are being achieved; the Cognitive System processes all the necessary information, and the Knowledge Domain provides the content."

Marzano, R. J. (2000), **Designing a new taxonomy of educational objectives,** Thousand Oaks, CA: Corwin Press, as found in Intel Education Initiative, (2007) Intel Corporation. Designing Effective Projects: Thinking Skills Frameworks, Marzano's New Taxonomy

3."I believe that if we listen to them (the Net Geners) and engage them, their culture of interaction, collaboration, and enablement will drive economic and social development and prepare this shrinking planet for a more secure, fair, and prosperous future. We can learn how to avoid and manage the dark side – a predictable thing with any new communications medium – more effectively."

Tapscott, Don (2009), GrownUp Digital, Tapscott, Don. Grown Up Digital, How the Net Generation is Changing Your World. McGraw Hill Co., New York: p. 13

4. "In education they (net generation) are forcing a change in the model of pedagogy from a teacher-focused approach based on instruction to a student-focused model based on collaboration."

Tapscott, Don (2009), GrownUp Digital, Tapscott, Don. Grown Up Digital, How the Net Generation is Changing Your World. McGraw Hill Co., New York

5."Instead of watching the clock like in school, they lose track of time -- arriving early, working into the evenings, on weekends and even school holidays – they are in the "flow." They learn to ask their own questions, uncover problems, propose solutions, and follow their explorations wherever they may lead. They present their final documentary, to public audiences of friends, family, teachers, and community members. Their work is validated in all its richness and creativity not with a single number or letter grade, but as it should be: through community appreciation, questioning, conversation and reflection."

The educational Video Center, 120 West 30th Street, 7th Floor, New York, NY, 10001,

info@evc.org,
http://www.evc.org/about/philosophy

Chapter 9: No Chapter, to challenge left-brainers.

1. No references either.

Chapter 10: Agents of change needed now. Peace achieved through education.

1. The 2006 PISA science assessment explores the relevance and importance that students attach to scientific issues in questions posed alongside those that test their cognitive abilities. Moreover, the ALL survey has experimented with assessing individuals' ability to co-operate with others, working in teams, although so far it has been difficult to translate this into a workable assessment within an international survey.

THE DEFINITION AND SELECTION OF KEY COMPETENCIES, Executive Summary, DeSeCo Project, www.oecd.org/edu/statistics/deseco, www.deseco.admin.ch

2. On the one hand, it was necessary to acknowledge how even common values can be interpreted differently in different cultures. On the other hand, those involved in the DeSeCo Project pointed out that certain countries have been able to identify common values even while acknowledging their differences. The project was

able to identify an agreed set of fundamental ideals with which a framework of key competencies needs to be compatible. This reflects a commonality of aspiration while accepting a diversity of application.

Reports from: Austria, Belgium, Denmark, Finland, France, Germany, the Netherlands, New Zealand, Norway, Sweden, Switzerland and the United States in the Final report in 2003: *Key Competencies for a Successful Life and a Well-Functioning Society* Dominique Simone Rychen and Laura Hersh Salganik (eds.)

Hogrefe & Huber, Göttingen, DeSeCo Project, www.oecd.org/edu/statistics/deseco, www.deseco.admin.ch, Mep_interieur 27/05/05 9:17 P.19

3. Globalization and modernization are creating an increasingly diverse and interconnected world. To make sense of and function well in this world, individuals need for example to master changing technologies and to make sense of large amounts of available information. They also face collective challenges as societies – such as balancing economic growth with environmental sustainability, and prosperity with social equity. In these contexts, the competencies that individuals need to meet their goals have become more complex, requiring more than the mastery of certain narrowly defined skills.

THE DEFINITION AND SELECTION OF KEY COMPETENCIES, Executive Summary, **DeSeCo Project,** www.oecd.org/edu/statistics/deseco,

4."Futurist Marsha Rhea writes about schools as the logical laboratory for learning together how to face challenges at a scale and complexity the world has never seen before. "We live in a time of split-second opportunities and threats.   We could just as easily fall into a feared future as stay on track for an expected future.   For a preferred future, we need to do much better than simply stay in step with rapid technological and evolutionary advances.   Anticipatory learning gives us the learning and skills to shape our future in complex and interdependent times."

Rhea. M. (2005) Anticipate the World You Want: Learning for Alternative Futures. Scarecrow Education, Lanham, MD, as reprinted in: Vision, 2021, Provocative Forecasts of Uncertainty and Opportunity, The institute for Alternative Futures, Partnership for 21st Century Skills, copyright 2007

5. As global education researchers David Baker and Gerald LeTendre observed, "A powerful modern ideology is that society itself is a project, and one of the fundamental parts of the project is to use education to achieve society." They see this ideology driving continuous reform across many nations. As nations work to keep pace with one another in a global community, they will gravitate more toward public policies that make social welfare a priority.

Vision, 2021, Provocative Forecasts of Uncertainty and Opportunity, The institute for Alternative Futures, Partnership for 21st Century Skills, copyright 2007,Baker, DP. And LeTendre, GK (2005) Op.cit.

6. "It is obvious that different people think about the same things in different ways."

Robinson, Sir Ken, (2009) The Element, Viking Penguin Group, (USA) Incorporated, 375 Hudson St. N.Y., N.Y., P. 96

World Class

About the Authors

Françoise Piron was born and raised in Geneva, Switzerland. She is the daughter of a French mother and a Belgian father. Piron has been teaching French at South Jefferson CSD, Adams, NY, for the last 25 years. Her undergraduate education took place in Geneva, and she received a Masters in Education (ITMM, Instructional Technology and Media Management) from SUNY Potsdam. She is a member of many professional organizations, including NYSAFLT, AATF, the LOTE Model Schools committee, NYSUT and NYSCATE. She is a Turnkey Trainer for her area and has been an item writer and consultant at the State Education Department for the NYS French Regents Exams and the NYS French Language Proficiency Exams since 1990. Piron has presented numerous workshops in the field of foreign languages at both local and statewide professional conferences. Since 2008, Piron has been the co-teacher of, "I am a Citizen of the World, a course in Media Literacy," designed by Mary Ellen Shevalier.

She has co-presented the course at numerous venues, including SUNY Oswego and NECC (National Educational Computing Conference) in San Diego, CA. Piron is the author of the published article, "Nine Steps to Diversity: Combining Art, French, and Technology in a Collaborative Journey and a Multi-layered Project", in the NYSAFLT Annual Meeting series no. 23, 2006. Piron is the recipient of two awards, the "ISE, Language Matters" Award (2009) and the Dorothy Ludwig Memorial Award for outstanding service to the foreign language teaching profession (2010). She is a firm believer in teaching children rather than teaching subject matter. She proudly emphasizes global equality in all aspects of her professional and personal life.

Mary Ellen Kalil Shevalier is a native of Syracuse, NY and has been a resident of Henderson, NY with her husband Mark, for 30 years. She holds a dual B.F.A. from Syracuse University in Fine Arts and Synaesthetic Education, a MFA and an Educational Administration degree from SUNY@ Oswego. She has been an art educator for the past 28 years. Shevalier has been a strong advocate for holistic education at the local, national, and international levels for which she has received several distinctions throughout her professional career. She is a member of many professional organizations that span the areas of educational administration, national education association, technology, English, and art.

Shevalier is a three time recipient of the outstanding teacher of the year award, respectively in the areas of art, dance, and technology. She has received the Disney Salutes the American Teacher Award as one of five top art educators in the country and one of sixty overall top educators in the nation. Her ideas about 21st century education and educational reform have been published in the following: SIGAdmin Fall newsletter, 2009; The *Edward Austin Sheldon, The Newsletter of SUNY Oswego School of Education; and Team Sheldon, Vol. 16, Issue 1, Spring 2009.* Shevalier is *the* designer of a 21st century media literacy curriculum entitled: "I am a Citizen of the World." She has presented this work at local, national, and international organizations including the following: The National Education Computer Conference, San Diego, CA; the Mega-Conference and International Technology Showcase; the NYSSBA Conference; and the Phi Delta Kappa Organization. Shevalier profoundly believes in the importance of education as the single most powerful tool to heal our society and our world.

World Class

Please visit our class website:

http://www.spartanpride.org/webpages/citizen/index.cfm

Contact the authors at:

worldclassbook@gmail.com